Kundalini Awakening Mastery

Discover Third Eye Opening, Psychic Development Awareness, Chakras, Reiki Healing, and Empathy to Achieve Higher Consciousness

Bodhi Fox

2021 All rights reserved. This book or parts thereof may not be reproduced in any form, stored in any retrieval system, or transmitted in any form by any means—electronic, mechanical, photocopy, recording, or otherwise—without prior written permission of the publisher, except as provided by United States of America copyright law. For permission requests, write to the publisher, at "Attention: Permissions Coordinator," at the address below.

Table of Contents

Introduction

Chapter 1: Yoga Psychology and Western Psychology: A Comparison

Distinctions in Yoga

Yogic and Vedic Psychology

Patanjali's Philosophy

Western Psychology

The Thin Line

Applying Yoga Psychology into Western Culture

Chapter 2: Basics of Kundalini

What Is the Meaning of Kundalini?

How Kundalini Yoga Is Helpful in Our Lives

The Basics of Breathing in Kundalini Yoga

Kundalini Yoga and the Basics of Mantras

The Basics of Kriyas in Kundalini Yoga

The Basics of Mudras in Kundalini Yoga

The Basics of Meditations in Kundalini Yoga

Chapter 3: History of Kundalini

India: A Possible Birthplace

Egyptian Civilization

The Chinese Concept

Other Traditions

Modern Culture

Chapter 4: Kundalini and the Ego
The Death of the Ego
The Awakening of Kundalini

Chapter 5: Benefits of Kundalini
Amplifies Energy
Boosts Body Positivity
Cognitive Improvements
Enlightens Spiritually
Enriches Empathy
Improves Charisma
Increases Creativity
Inner Peace
Makes you Mindful
Relieves Stress and Anxiety
Strengthens Body & Mind
Treats Addictions
Welcoming Well-Being

Chapter 6: A Guide to Chakras
The 7 Chakras of Life
Why Balancing Chakras Is Important
Awakening Chakras
Benefits of Awakening Chakras

Chapter 7: Pranayama, Drishti, Asanas, Mantras and Mudras
Pranayama

Drishti
Asanas
Mantras
Mudras

Chapter 8: Kundalini and Meditation
Kundalini Yoga Meditation
Benefits of Kundalini Meditation
Featured Meditations
Yogic Science

Chapter 9: Different Kundalini Exercises
How to Prepare Before Kundalini Exercises
The Elements of Kundalini Yoga
Different Kundalini Exercises

Chapter 10: Kundalini Awakening and Its Effects
What is Kundalini Awakening?
A Brief History of Kundalini Awakening
The Philosophy of Kundalini Awakening
How is Kundalini Awakened?
What Enables Kundalini Awakening?
Effects and Signs of an Awakened Kundalini
Dangers of Kundalini Awakening

Chapter 11: How to Support Your Kundalini Awakening
Why Can Kundalini Awakening Get Intense?
Supporting the Process of a Mild Kundalini Awakening

Supporting an Intense Kundalini Awakening

Handling Kundalini Awakening Based on the Symptoms

Chapter 12: The Third Eye and Third Eye Opening

The Relation between Third Eye and Kundalini Awakening

The Ajna Chakra

How to Activate the Third Eye

Meditation

Seek Help from Your Dreams

Use Healing Crystals

Third Eye Affirmations

Chapter 13: Reiki Healing and Its Relation to Awakening

How is Kundalini Awakening Related to Reiki Healing?

Is Reiki Effective?

Health Benefits of Reiki

How Is Reiki Carried Out?

Reiki Techniques

Who Is It Meant For? What Can One Expect?

Reiki for a Self-Practitioner

Conclusion

References

Introduction

Kundalini. You might have heard this word before, as it is often used in yogic and psychic practices. Kundalini refers to indomitable energy that every person possesses but often remains dormant or un-accessed. With an active Kundalini, one can explore the many facets of the spiritual world by feeling more aware of one's senses, conscious of the world around, and energized to take on daily life. It not only reanimates your soul but also galvanizes you to "see" beyond the tangible realm. Energy, which translates to "Shakti", should be pushed towards the head and transported above it. Since the energy of Lord Shiva resonates from the head, the practice to awaken Kundalini should be effective enough to reach the top of the head, also known as the crown chakra. This is where real enlightenment transpires.

Kundalini is a form of life force that expends energy and creative power to amplify one's consciousness and elevate their overall well-being. Some yogis hypothesize that one's inner fire and passion can also be deemed their Kundalini. In essence, Kundalini energy refers to a coil of energy that is accumulated at the bottom of the spine. While some people may have dormant Kundalini energy, others may experience its intense effect. An analogy suggests that just like you need to turn a switch to obtain light, you have to awaken your Kundalini energy by flipping the switch through various practices.

While Kundalini is deemed feminine, the masculine energy of Lord Shiva creates an intrinsic amalgamation of the two energies and pushes you into a state of divinity. Simply put, if accessed correctly, you can enter into a phase of pure ecstasy. As you feel the energy rising over your body through the nadis and into your head, you get to experience a sublime transformation in your body, mind, and soul.

The advent of Kundalini can be attributed to the Upanishads, in which several ideas about Hinduism and essential philosophical ideas have been narrated. In fact, Kundalini has been avidly practiced in both Hinduism and Buddhism for centuries. The esoteric arms of both realms oblige them to perform "tantra," which refers to the use and/or application of mystical texts, beliefs, and practices. Kundalini is also practiced by several other sects, albeit under different names. For instance, it is known as Shekhinah in Kabbalah. The serpent is a symbol often associated with Kundalini, as many ancient texts depict the energy to visually resemble a coiled snake resting at the bottom of a person's spine, ready to unfurl itself through the body once the energy is correctly unlocked.

To awaken and energize your Kundalini, you must go through several practices to ignite your inner fire and feel "refreshed". This phenomenon is known as Kundalini awakening. A high number of individuals practicing yoga and healing techniques to activate their Kundalini swear by its life-changing effects that resonate in every aspect of their life. Activating your Kundalini will feel like the energy is being emitted by flowing, liquid fire- stimulating and invigorating.

As previously mentioned, the practices you undertake can either gently or vigorously awaken the sleeping snake. The energy produced will then seep into your body and transpose itself in a wavy curve, similar to how a serpent slithers on a surface. It starts curving its way upwards from the bottom, spirals into the gut, and ultimately moves towards the head through the heart, thereby energizing the body and mind. Since our chakras are located throughout the entire body, the energy impacts every one of those areas and balances the entire system. From the root chakra to the crown chakra, every element experiences an electric effect that rejuvenates one's physical, mental, emotional, and spiritual health. It is believed that our bodies have energy pipes, or "nadis," and driving energy through these pipes can impact our consciousness and possibly expand it.

As a mode of clarification, how one uses and handles snake poison can either save someone's life or kill them. Similarly, the way you activate and energize your Kundalini can impact your life and well-being accordingly. Due to its complex nature, Kundalini awakening often receives criticism since not many people are able to fully elucidate the enigma of this powerful force. However, with the right practices and patience, you can easily unleash its true potential and creative power. As mentioned, if perceived reprehensibly, Kundalini awakening can destroy you too. Just like the snake poison, you must handle it justly to experience coexistence and duality.

If practiced correctly, certain rituals can awaken Kundalini and place you on the path of enlightenment. Due to this, the awakening itself not just the final goal, but the spiritual journey itself is crucial. Note that the process takes time. Most people manage to push the energy right from their root chakra (Muladhara) up to the third chakra (Manipur), which is located between the breastbone and belly button. It can take a lifetime for individuals who are not fully determined or patient with themselves.

Practices used to awaken one's Kundalini range from low-key rituals, such as changing one's diet and listening to certain types of music, to more high-intensity practices like deep meditation and performing mudras. It is also believed that sexual activity can steadily provoke one's Kundalini energy to wake up and stay active for a prolonged period of time. This transcendent urge comes from the energizing effect of Kundalini that can successfully convert biological instincts into something more plausible and desirable. Some forms of movement (Shakti dances) can also help. Furthermore, the act of Shaktipat- transferring positive energy from the guru to the pupil-is also an emphatic way to awaken one's Kundalini energy. This act is usually performed by chanting certain mantras or by touching the location of the third eye.

In this book, we will cover every aspect of Kundalini awakening and its ability to manifest positive energy, namely psychic development awareness, third eye opening, Reiki healing, the chakra system, and empathy in order to access your true spiritual realm. Once you master the intricate art of Kundalini awakening, you can explore new and unseen dimensions that can completely change your life and put your mind at ease. You will also feel a surge in your creativity, intuition, knowledge, and appreciation for life.

Read on to garner the concept of Kundalini awakening in its entirety and manifest positive energy to change your life along with experiencing cosmic consciousness.

Chapter 1: Yoga Psychology and Western Psychology: A Comparison

Yoga has been in existence for centuries and is still widely practiced and praised all around the world. That being said, its potential benefits have still not managed to garner enough attention in some regions of the world. Those who are raised with a more practical and logical approach fail to see past the pragmatic realm, which makes them more skeptical about the entire spirituality model.

Simply put, yoga is the concept of connecting or uniting the mind, body, and soul to feel enlightenment and heighten consciousness beyond the tangible realm. Individuals introduced to the concept of yoga often misinterpret the true essence behind this practice, which leads to poor results.

When diagnosing an ailment to one's physical or mental health, medical practitioners often ignore the crux of the problem and focus just on treating the visibly affected area and its accompanying symptoms. Yoga, on the other hand, works on preventing these health issues from occurring in the first place. This major difference is two distinct mindsets, which are either Eastern or Western-based. Even though the East and West seem to have different approaches to healing ailments, they can be amalgamated to form a tenacious treatment model.

In this chapter, we will draw distinct parallels between western and eastern psychology to understand the concepts in-depth and how they can be applied in the real world.

Distinctions in Yoga

Even though the concept of yoga differs around the world, we can effectively draw some common ground around various cultures and religions. For instance, Buddhism and Hinduism both practice yoga, but the significances of said practices differ based on cultural differences. While India is a land of supernatural life patterns and mystical stories, China has a much more practical approach to yoga. Moreover, tradition in many Chinese regions tends to separate the religious aspect of yoga from the practice itself. For instance, it is very common for yogis in said regions to be agnostic, while others may either be atheists or Buddhists.

Yoga is comprised of six different aspects, which are Bhakti yoga (devotion), Raja yoga (royal meditation), Hatha yoga (body), Tantra yoga (Kundalini and chakra powers), Jhana yoga (wisdom and knowledge), and Karma yoga (service). In the modern world, all forms of yoga are recognized as physical and mental exercises for one's well-being. The Brahma-Atman (universe and spirit) equation, Sanskaras, renunciation, Shanti, Sat, and self-discipline also form an integral part of this system.

Yogic and Vedic Psychology

Psychology or psychotherapy can be perceived and implemented through distinct paradigms that collectively aim to enhance one's mental well-being. One such facet is yogic psychology or psychoanalysis that helps you become more aware of your actions and thoughts in each instance. At times, we absent-mindedly perform an activity or think an obscure thought. This is when yoga psychology steps in. Once you start observing yourself performing tasks and focus on how you carry them out, you can steadily step into the domain of yoga psychology. This concept dictates that there are two distinct entities involved in this process, the first one being the doer (operative principle) and the second the observer (cognitive principle). According to yogic texts, the doer is considered Shakti, and the observer is personified as Shiva.

The operative principle implies that you, as a person, are not just defined by your thoughts but also an integral part of consciousness, which helps you observe and fulfill the cognitive principle required in this practice. Karma is also another significant principle often used in yogic psychology. This term reflecting cause and effect is often ciphered using the idiom, "you reap what you sow". In essence, karma translates to "action" in the Sanskrit language. The collection of actions you endure throughout your lifetime is directly related to karma. You must look into the consequences of your actions to truly fathom the concept of karma.

Whether it's a positive or negative situation, every action will have an equal reaction, either from your end or otherwise. These reactions are imprinted in your mind like memories and can remain there for a lifetime. These impressions (also known as "samskaras" in Sanskrit) can resurface at times, either by being instigated or completely out of the blue. The samskaras in one's mind are formed due to strenuous or negative past events and eventually become part of the unconscious mind. If in any situation, one of the impressions strengthens, your reaction will directly affect the action. For example, if you are planning to go out for lunch with your friends but you suddenly remember a random negative incident that occurred a few years ago, your reaction to this sudden unearthed memory will change the entire course of your actions throughout your lunch date. In other words, your samskara will impact your life decisions. Your karma has and will keep impacting your samskara, which is regarded as the root cause that floats in your mind. This, in turn, can impact your behavior and mindset in the long run.

It is believed that one's samskaras stay in the mind even after a person dies. Yogic philosophy stresses the concept of reincarnation and insists your past life's actions and thoughts will somehow affect your next life. All your actions or karmas will impact your samskaras and vice versa in some cases. The witnessing entity, which is the soul, remains the same and just transfers to a new vessel in the next life. The soul and mind carry the same samskaras and can portray them—either vaguely or robustly—through new karmas or actions. This is why yogis believe in expelling the accumulated samskaras that may affect them in the next life.

An effective way to do so is meditation. When you meditate, you concentrate on your breathing pattern and chant mantras, which bring you closer to your thoughts and help you differentiate between the soul and mind (which are often perceived as one). The vibrations in the mantras help you get closer to your consciousness, as well as enhance self-awareness. The witnessing entity in you can be awakened by meditation. In a way, it helps you escape your thoughts and divert your attention towards your soul and consciousness.

Once you get rid of those attachments, you can effectively dismiss your samskaras as well.

Madhu Vidya, roughly translated to "Honey Knowledge", is also another facet related to yogic psychology that is connected to supreme consciousness. This concept states that your actions are a result of supreme energy and not your own conscious mind, which obliges you to surrender the reactions. You are, in fact, a medium or instrument that allows those thoughts and actions to be expressed. This gives you a sense of freedom and lets you stay away from attachments, which is one of the ultimate goals of yogic philosophy. Various attributes that separate individuals and give them an identity are believed to stem from samskaras as well. While some are calmer and content with life, others are more ambitious and artistic. If you remove these attributes and tendencies, all individuals will be equal.

Patanjali's Philosophy

On a minute scale, yoga helps one heal and stay more aware of their surroundings. This consciousness allows them to take more control of their life and environment. But, on a larger scale, yogis seek this practice to attain "moksha" or liberation from this world.

Patanjali's Yoga Sutras, better known as the Ashtanga Yoga System (Eight Limbs of Yoga), teaches us a method to attain liberation or moksha through eight steps.

1. Yama - Moral Vows

The first limb teaches us to take moral vows and discipline ourselves to keep peace and maintain steady interaction with others around us. This helps us stay positive and reduces stress as well. In a way, you get to be more aware of the world around you and ensure that it is free of vices. The five Yamas, or vows, are- Satya (truthfulness), Ahimsa (non-violence), Aparigraha (non-greed or non-hoarding), Brahmacharya (right use of energy), and Asteya (non-stealing). This limb also emphasizes the fact that the essential benefits of yoga cannot be achieved simply by practicing breathing techniques and meditation in a closed room for a few minutes but by being more truthful and kind to yourself and others around you.

2. Niyama - Moral Duties

The second limb, Niyama, represents a set of moral duties or rules that one must follow to build character and feel closer to their true self. "Ni" means "within", which directly relates to cleansing from inside. The five Niyamas are- santosha (contentment), svadhyaya (self-reflection), saucha (cleanliness), Ishvara Pranidhana (surrendering to the highest power), and tapas (burning desires). By practicing these moral duties, one can steadily move forward on the path of enlightenment and get closer to liberation. These duties also affect our sheaths or "Koshas", which are used to slowly cleanse our spirit and help us attain truth.

3. Asana - Posture

This limb focuses on the physical act of seating oneself comfortably to improve posture and avoid aches in joints. While the literal meaning of asana refers to seating, a set of asanas or postures can be practiced by standing and bending your body to improve your physical state. In essence, Patanjali emphasizes the posture, "sthira sukham asanam," which means sitting comfortably and motionless. Other asanas that can accompany this limb are Virasana (hero pose) and Padmasana (lotus pose).

4. Pranayama - Breathing Techniques

The fourth limb focuses on the way we breathe. "Prana" translates to life source or energy and denotes the energy around us. The essence of staying alive through our breath is primarily focused on using the fourth limb. The word "Pranayama" translates to "breath control", which if practiced correctly, can lead to tranquility and breath liberation. While some feel more controlled when practicing Pranayama, others feel freer when controlling their breath. Certain breathing techniques, like Kapalbhati and Chandra Bhadana, are included.

5. Pratyahara - Withdrawal of Senses

Pratya means "withdrawing", and Ahara means "taking in". Collectively, it means taking in the senses surrounding us, which can be taste, smell, sound, sight, etc. In a way, this limb is connected to pranayama because we tend to sense our breathing during meditation. With utter concentration, we can focus on our breathing and shut down all the other things happening around us. This vaguely translates to the effect of withdrawing our senses as we tend to immerse into our minds and souls when meditating.

6. Dharana - Concentration

This limb is loosely connected to Pranayama and Pratyahara as it emphasizes the essence of deep concentration and staying in the moment. Once you withdraw your senses, you can shift your focus to your mind. Several practices are used to build Dharana, such as breathing techniques, visualization practices, and Tratak-candle gazing.

7. Dhyana - Absorption through Meditation

This is the stage where you get deeply involved in meditation and are completely "absorbed". This is the actual state of mediation wherein your mind and soul can become one. The true significance of mediation is not realizing your current state and letting the event occur as a spontaneous action.

8. Samadhi - Enlightenment

The last limb, which is the significant path to liberation, eternal bliss, or enlightenment, is called Samadhi. Once you sort yourself out in the outer world and the relationships you form in it, you focus on your inner self (as represented by the second limb). You can thereby step on the path of enlightenment using the other limbs. Samadhi means realization; the one who attains Samadhi can see the real world that lies in front of them. Do not mistake eternal bliss with floating away or literally escaping the world. In essence, Samadhi refers to the ability to ascend without causing pain or disturbance to the soul and mind. You can view the world more justly, free of all obligations and greed. You will no longer attach yourself to anyone or anything. You will be free of judgment, negativity, and vices.

Samadhi is, however, a temporary state and needs practice and determination to turn into a permanent one. The mind needs to be completely purified and free of attachments before it can attain a state of freedom, liberation, or Mukti.

It is essential to learn the metaphysics of these eight limbs as it can effectively draw parallels between the state of ignorance or imbalance with liberation. The three gunas (characteristics) of an individual are sattva (goodness), rajas (passion), and tamas (destructive). All three are present in every individual in varying degrees. The way they are proportioned and balanced also determines an individual's psychological disposition. While psychologists study the signs that triggered this imbalance, yoga focuses on balancing all gunas to keep an individual in their best state.

Western Psychology

The Western world greatly advocates self-improvement and mental well-being, which urges them to invest in mindful practices such as yoga and acupuncture. In fact, the self-improvement industry in the West is valued at billions of dollars, which is steadily increasing with the global decline in mental health. Even though psychology is diverse and an extremely wide subject, you can still narrow it down to separate fields, with the yogic approach being one.

The difference also originates from the way people are brought up in the West versus the East. While the East teaches a child to develop a good character by teaching them ethics, the West focuses on how to act in any situation. Even though both individuals may appear benevolent and generous, the individual with good character will act more righteously.

A heightened sense of insecurity may somehow lead an individual to seek spirituality and search for God, which is reinforced by the social norms of the environment one grows up in. If you are a bit skeptical about the positive impact of yoga, your friends or family who have highly benefited from this practice can easily inspire you to give it a shot.

The Thin Line

While western psychology classifies the mind as an extension of the body, Vedic psychology claims that the body and mind are, in fact, a combined extension of the soul. The latter believes that an individual and their well-being are incomplete without their soul and spirit. In fact, the soul is one's true guiding power; it is your walking stick or guiding star that points you in the right direction and supports you as you endure the journey.

In the modern world, any form of physical and mental illness is treated by focusing on the symptoms instead of diagnosing the patient's body and mental state in a holistic approach. Doctors and medical professionals focus on what's wrong instead of what is or what may go right. This also leads to breaking the patient's case by focusing on a particular body part or area of treatment instead of looking at it as a whole. In other words, they do not treat the issue by connecting the mind to the body but focusing on the body parts that are affected by the issue.

On the other hand, yoga is considered a holistic approach that treats the issue inside out and prevents it from occurring in the first place. The stressor that may cause any illness is treated from the beginning, stressors that can drain one's physical and mental health. Those susceptible to any mental illness are prescribed yoga or meditation practices.

Simply put, yoga treats the root or crux of the problem instead of working on just the symptoms of any ailment. In the latter case, the person is already suffering from the illness, which can be avoided with yoga practices.

Applying Yoga Psychology into Western Culture

While most people who are introduced to yoga are open to trying it out, some still find it difficult to believe in the effectiveness of this spiritual approach. The only way to get them on board is by explaining the true concepts, philosophies, and mechanisms of yoga and relevant spiritual practices. The most effective way to treat any issue is by combining the medicinal science approach with the supreme power of yoga. You may think that modeling this holistic approach can be quite challenging, whereas, in reality, it is much simpler than one can imagine.

Recall the eight components of yoga (Ashtanga) mentioned earlier. It states that by consistently practicing these eight limbs, one can find the path to enlightenment. The approach to treating a mental health issue in the western world is similar; the therapist or doctor follows a set of steps that helps them decipher a patient's problem and treat their signs. Issues like anxiety, OCD, depression, PTSD, etc., are effectively treated using cognitive-behavioral therapy, which is an extensively studied therapeutic solution to treat mental health problems. Basically, the patients are compelled to change the way they think, and the practitioners help them face their fears and guide them through the process of healing. By acknowledging their thoughts, the patient can, in turn, change their feelings. With time, this can steadily treat their mental problem as well.

Some forms of cognitive-behavioral therapy also state that the person's environment and physical body can impact their mental health, which can heighten the effect of the problem.

One major challenge that we must consider when combining both practices is the linear design of the western clinical approach and the multi-faceted model of the yogic eastern form of healing. While the eight components of yoga are further divided into several components (making it an extensive approach), the medical model is much easier to accept. More importantly, it yields results much faster. However, if you are a patient, the yogic approach can fix the crux of the problem and impact your behavior as well. You can treat the physical distress that can reduce signs related to any mental health issue. During yoga, you are instigated to focus on your mind and be more aware, which can instantly change your behavior.

As mentioned earlier, the things you observe and the type of content you reflect on can majorly affect your conscious thinking as well. This implies that yoga and relevant practices can be labeled as original or a more authentic way of conducting cognitive-behavioral therapy. The quality of insights and thoughts you achieve after practicing yoga can be efficiently implemented in a western mentality. However, you may need professional help to design a robust model, as they can provide essential feedback and guidance needed to make the treatment more potent. While the western blueprint can benefit from preventive techniques and fixing issues from the root, the yogic realm can lean on relational and communication skills. This symbiotic relationship can be supremely beneficial for all individuals on the physical, mental, emotional, and spiritual scales. Needless to say, it can reduce the number of illnesses and disorders humans suffer from on a global scale.

Chapter 2: Basics of Kundalini

Every life has vibrant energy within it. Not just the living, but the non-living things are also comprised of energy. Therefore, everyone and everything people interact with is pure energy. Kundalini, or the Serpent Power or the Inner woman, is a form of energy mentioned in several esoteric traditions. Its divine form is coiled at the base of our spine. Ever since our birth, it's been there – dormant.

You can think of it as a coiled cable wire that is unable to locate a power socket to complete the connection. As per the ancient texts, this mystical energy is personified in a double-ended snake that sits coiled at the bottom of your spine. This snake, if awakened, can either give its bearer the power to become more creative or disruptive. Hinduism uses a snake to depict this pure form of energy because snake venom has that same dualistic potential of either healing or destroying.

In the current world, many yoga enthusiasts try to locate this pure energy by practicing various forms like tantra, hatha yoga and Kundalini yoga. However, the concept of Kundalini has been recorded within the Upanishads, sacred Sanskrit texts covering all the philosophical ideas and concepts of Hinduism. Many of these ideas can also be found in Buddhism. This energy can also be found in several other traditions, with varying names. For instance, in Kabbalah, it's known as Shekinah.

Throughout your life, you'll witness challenges, hardships and triumphs. To overcome them all, Kundalini aids you in reacting to varying situations with a neutral perspective. It guides you throughout all the scenarios with calmness, ensuring that you are at your best self while dealing with the ups and downs in your life. It's said that the very first yoga ever developed was based on Kundalini yoga, which helped the practitioners heal themselves. Some scientific results support this mystical concept, which has been proven to activate certain parts of the brain, generating a balanced control and increasing awareness. With time, practicing certain movements and controlled breathing, this Kundalini can escalate your energetic awareness and help enhance your cellular bonding present throughout the nervous system.

What Is the Meaning of Kundalini?

In Sanskrit, Kundalini refers to a "coiled snake". One of the core beliefs of Hinduism is that the pure form of energy is generated at the foundation of the spine. With Kundalini, one can "uncoil the snake" and link to this mystical energy present in abundance within the body.

When Kundalini was first created, it was linked to the scientific study of spiritual and energy philosophy. In the past, it was imperative for the royal family members and aristocrats to be well-educated about the science behind Kundalini. It wasn't until the mid-20th century that Yogi Bhajan introduced this exotic art to the west. With his influence, this beautiful concept evolved into spiritual practice, blending ancient knowledge with modern means of practice. With his help, Kundalini yoga became more accessible to anyone who is willing to learn it.

How Kundalini Yoga Is Helpful in Our Lives

Every Kundalini practitioner uses it as a tool to obtain a complete life with boundless love, joy, calmness, and lightness. Kundalini yoga is not only capable of helping you generate awareness about your body's geometrical shape but can also awaken your vision about its effects on your body's movement, emotions, and energy. By knowing all these characteristics of your body, you are able to act and react more efficiently and quickly.

In terms of Yoga, the energy in everybody is locked, which disrupts its flow – causing the connection between the mind and body to remain severed. As a result, we cannot attain the full potential of our bodies. When you practice Kundalini Yoga, it pulls the energy trapped at the base of your spine through your crown's roof and out of the body, helping to generate an energy flow. This helps in creating a steady form of energy that maintains a balance in your chakras or energy centers.

To master Kundalini yoga, you have to understand its technicalities, which include mudras, meditation forms, kriyas, mantras, and breathwork. Learning all these will help you understand this divine art better, allowing you to churn its benefits for your overall well-being. In the beginning, it might be a little weird to practice these breathing, postures, and chanting techniques. However, with commitment, you can get the most out of this divine practice. Besides consistency, you will have to keep an open mind to the mystical ideas revolving around Kundalini and its foundation.

The Basics of Breathing in Kundalini Yoga

Breathing is the most basic habit that enables every living thing to live. It might feel like one of the simplest things to do, and yet, it's also one of the most complex things to grasp in yoga. Depth, frequency, and pattern are all factors that contribute to the biorhythms of our bodies. We subconsciously breathe most of the time in our lives, and that's the main difference between pranayama and breathing.

What is Pranayama?

Pranayama or pranayam refers to the science of conscious breathing, which is done by controlling one's prana (Sanskrit word for "life force") by applying specific methods. While breathing is responsible for keeping us alive, pranayama can offer a better quality of life. While prana is considered the life force, the concept of Ayama depicts the means to lengthen or regulate a person's prana. Together, pranayama is a way of working in the scope of prana.

Think of your body like a candle wick with your mind acting as the glow around a burning flame. Prana acts as the vital energy or life force needed to keep our physical body and its delicate layers alive.

You may have heard of the term aura and how it presents as a field of color around a person. The energy of prana acts the same way, flowing through energy channels known as nadis and energy-dissipating centers called chakras. The quality and quantity of the flow of prana through chakras and nadis determine how well an individual's mind functions.

With a high level of prana, the energy flow remains steady, smooth, and consistent, which keeps the mind enthusiastic, positive, and calm. If an individual does not have a good prana level, it will result in blockages of various energy channels. This causes a disrupted prana flow, leading to conflicts, tensions, uncertainties, fear, worries, and anger. All these problems first develop within the body and flow outward towards the surface with time. This results in various forms of physical and mental illnesses.

So, to ensure that the body functions optimally, the flow of prana has to be consistent.

What Do You Mean by "Natural" Breathing?

To breathe naturally, one inhales, which causes the navel point to move outward, and exhaling makes the navel point move back inwards. Furthermore, natural breathing enlists the use of the nose, which acts as an air filter we breathe through. Many individuals practice incorrect breathing techniques subconsciously, with the belly drawing inwards when inhaling and vice versa. This causes the lungs to take in less air, which is not healthy. In Kundalini Yoga, the basics of breathing naturally are one of the most important practices that help release the energy flow throughout the body. Improving how you breathe is the key to strengthening your mind-body connection.

Other than conforming to incorrect breathing patterns, some individuals often breathe erratically through the upper chest, which results in shallow breathing and an underflow through the chakras. Moreover, correct breathing is the gateway to an upgraded consciousness. Due to stress, people often practice shallow breathing unknowingly. Doing it continuously causes their nervous systems to weaken, making their bodies prone to unwanted medical conditions. Due to emotional stress, trauma can accumulate in the muscular system. With proper breathing, this trauma can be released and eventually resolved.

In other words, the body is stiffened upon being emotionally distressed. The trauma building up causes the mind and body to become rigid to protect against the agitating forces. With natural breathing, the body corrects itself, loosening to the stress and evacuating the trauma by increasing the prana flow. As a result, you improve your vitality and overall well-being.

Frequency of Breathing

The key to sound breathing is to practice lowering its frequency to do more work inside our bodies. Decreasing frequency can help the body achieve greatness. In general, a normal male would have a breath frequency of 16 to 20 cycles (inhaling and exhaling session) in a minute. Similarly, a woman would have a frequency of 18 to 22 cycles in a minute. If the breathing frequency can be lowered to 8 cycles per minute, it would help relax the body considerably. It will help decrease the stress in the body, leading to the sharpening of the mental acuity, as there would be an increase in the engagement of the parasympathetic nervous system.

Advanced practitioners have been known to reducing this breathing cycle to an even more controlled frequency of up to 4 cycles per minute, which further increases sensitivity, clarity, and awareness. Achieving this level of breath frequency will heighten the coordination between pineal and pituitary glands, leading to a higher level of meditative state. Now, imagine the yogis who can achieve a breathing frequency of just 1 cycle per minute, which is also known as One-Minute Breath. That's where the body goes through mind-blowing changes.

With the One-Minute Breath technique, you inhale for 20 seconds, hold it for the next 20, and exhale it in the remaining 20 seconds. This practice causes optimal coordination between both brain hemispheres and curbs stress, anxiety, and fear for good. You will literally feel your complete body unified as a complete force of energy emanating from the divine aura of your being. However, mastering an intense level of breathing frequency like this is not everybody's cup of tea. It requires immense amounts of practice, consistency, determination, and patience.

Where to Proceed with Pranayama

We mentioned above that pranayama and other breathing exercises are not that easy because many individuals often feel dizzy when trying to control their breathing. If that happens to you, stop and take a step back. There's no shame in knowing your limits. You need to generate the capacity of breathing safely – not through force, but through regularity and time.

Long Deep Breathing

Every form of yoga and meditation involves a certain posture and breathing pattern that helps to release or generate a certain type of energy. Kundalini Yoga is no different. One of the most common ones that every beginner learns is the Long Deep Breath. It requires one to breathe deeply and slowly through the nose. To do it, you will need to expand your stomach outward when inhaling and contract it when exhaling for air.

Once you are good at Natural Breathing, you can start with Long, Deep Breathing. This type of breathing has several advantages, such as:

- Managing negativity

- Re-channeling and conditioning pain

- Breaking subconscious patterns

- Helping with emotional and physical healing

- Releasing energy meridians that are blocked

- Regulating pH

- Cleansing the blood

- Re-adjusting the electromagnetic field

- Improving intuition

- Pumping the spinal fluid to your brain

- Stimulating endorphins

- Preventing the toxins to build up in the lungs

- Increasing the prana flow

- Relaxing one's mind and body

To practice Long Deep Breathing, you will need to use the full capacity of your lungs' three chambers: clavicular (upper), chest (middle), and abdominal (lower). Fill up the lower or abdominal area with air by expanding the chest and lifting the top ribs. Exhale lower the ribs slowly and deflate the chest, exhaling the air from the top towards the abdomen area. The final stage involves exhaling from the abdomen, pulling your navel point in an attempt to connect it to the spinal point. It might feel challenging, for starters. So, an easier way to start practicing is by concentrating on the spine so that you can see and feel the lungs operating consistently.

Breath of Fire

Another technique that is revered by the majority of Kundalini Yoga practitioners is the Breath of Fire. To perform this correctly, you will have to breathe rapidly and consistently through the nose, causing a quick de- and inflating of the stomach to generate spurs of oxygen flow in the blood. Doing so will also help your electromagnetic field charge up. Using this Kundalini technique correctly can help you reduce stress. Breathing practices like these also involve certain postures that help the body feel more balanced while performing the techniques.

To begin, start in a seated position, and make sure to sit up straight. Place your palms facing upwards on your knees. If you like, you can place the hand on your stomach to feel the air rising and falling as you practice breathing. Use your nose to inhale, simultaneously feeling your belly protrude outwards. You don't have to hold your breath during this exercise, so make sure you exhale forcefully through the nose while rapidly contracting the muscles in your abdomen area. Keep inhaling and exhaling at equal cycles. Repeat the pattern at your own pace and comfort.

In Breath of Fire, you have to be consistent with passive inhaling and forceful exhaling. You also need to practice the breathing exercise often to get comfortable with it. Once you have built up a slow and steady rhythm, work on speeding up the breathing cycle. With every step, you'll get closer to reaching your optimal being. Make sure you use a loud and powerful force to exhale the air. It is important to consistently practice to start seeing results.

Other Pranayama Forms

Besides the above two popular techniques of pranayamas, you will find many more breathing forms in Kundalini Yoga. These include Vatskar Pranayam, Sitkari Pranayam, Whistle Breath, Lion Breath, Segmented Breath, Cannon Breath, Right and Left Nostril Breathing, Alternate Nostril Breathing, and Sitali Pranayam. It's great to know and practice them all so that you can attain as many benefits as you can from Kundalini Yoga.

Kundalini Yoga and the Basics of Mantras

Mantras are often confused with magic enchantments, as depicted in several forms of entertainment. Instead, mantras use sounds and chants to attain the power of signaling a chemical reaction in the body and mind. The chanting of mantras helps to channel the positive power present in various forms of mood, which could be sadness, joy, or happiness. This results in bringing prosperity, abundance, and peace to ourselves.

Furthermore, when you chant a mantra, you regulate your body to vibrate at a particular sound frequency, which elevates your mood to reach a higher level of vibration, leading to a clarified state of mind. Chanting mantras does not necessarily involve sitting in a cross-legged state. One can even use mantras when driving, sleeping, or doing chores. These sacred sounds release energy that fills the surroundings. You can find several types of mantras that are targeted at attaining specific forms of moods and clarities in life.

The Basics of Kriyas in Kundalini Yoga

Kriya is considered to be a collection of exercises and is used in any form of Yoga. When you chant, maintain a certain posture, or engage your body in a breathing technique, you are technically performing kriya. Kriya literally means "action", and it involves a certain set of actions that you perform with the intention to manifest one form out of another. Kriyas operate on all levels of spirit, body, and mind, creating the healthiest life that is complete with vitality. For example, balancing the Aura is a form of kriya exercise that lets you effectively and quickly elevate your energy, build your stamina, and shield your energy from disruptions.

The Basics of Mudras in Kundalini Yoga

Mudras refer to the positions of the hands while performing yoga that direct and lock energy into various portions of the brain. These mudras have been mapped by yogis over thousands of years, demonstrating how every form of hand placement is linked to various parts of the body and brain. One of the most basic forms is the finger-to-finger placement form, which, when executed correctly, helps with energy activation.

In Kundalini Yoga, the most common of the mudra forms is the Gyan Mudra, which uses the index fingers and thumb to trigger the knowledge within. To achieve this mudra, you have to apply pressure with your thumb to the index finger, activating various pressure points on the finger. The index finger is said to be lined with Jupiter, which depicts expansion in general. So, in this mudra form, you feel calm and receptive. It's a passive form of mudra that has great potential to help reduce stress.

There are countless mudras that are targeted at a number of ailments in your body and mind. For instance, you can use a form to open up your communication blocks, which can help you with your daily chores, stressful business meetings, your first date, or an exam. This mudra involves pressing the thumb pad onto your pinky's (Mercury) fingernail for a minute. It will help increase your self-confidence, letting you communicate with others more actively. Next, touch your thumb to your pinky finger lightly; this enables you to regulate your ego by channeling your energy to align with your disruptive mood.

The Basics of Meditations in Kundalini Yoga

Most of us are aware of meditation, which will let us awaken our senses to become more creative and active in life. In Kundalini Yoga, people meditate at various lengths to attain different results. For instance, meditating for 3 minutes can affect your body's blood circulation and electromagnetic field, while an 11 minutes long meditation session can help improve the glandular and nervous systems of the body. A more advanced meditation session of 31 minutes would help clear out the subconscious mind, improving the cellular rhythm of the body.

Kundalini Yoga meditation will help you understand how Kundalini awakening can make you feel and affect you emotionally, physically, and mentally. Furthermore, you will notice a boost in your energy, allowing your body to have higher stamina throughout your daily routine. You will also feel a rise in your energy during the times of day when you usually feel the most depleted or drained. With the power of Kundalini Yoga, you can revamp your spirit, coordination, and focus with an abundance of your energy.

Chapter 3: History of Kundalini

Although the practice of Kundalini started gaining popularity in the West during the early 70s, literature shows it has been around for at least five thousand years. Since most of the records about Kundalini teachings originate from ancient Hindu texts called the Upanishads, it's safe to assume this type of spiritual meditation was born in the Asian subcontinent of India. Besides this geographic area, evidence of Kundalini was found in scrolls of Ancient Egyptians, Chinese Dynasties, and Native Americans. Some Tibetan and African religions can be associated with Kundalini as well. In all these different cultures and through all the centuries, Kundalini surfaced under different names, yet the essence of its practice has always stayed the same. Whether it was faith in magic, deities, life after death, or transcendence, the knowledge of Kundalini was present in many religious and spiritual doctrines. Due to its spiritual nature, Kundalini was often misunderstood, and until the 20th century, it was only practiced in secrecy. This chapter focuses on how the practice of Kundalini was molded by history from the time it was first recorded until today.

India: A Possible Birthplace

The exact origins of Kundalini are still unknown to this day. The earliest evidence in history about an individual practicing Kundalini was found in the Indus Valley dated to around 3000 BCE. As the practice of Kundalini has always been passed down as oral tradition from master to student, some unwritten practices may date back even further in history. The civilization of Indus Valley was known to have an exceptionally high level of spirituality. Their history was recorded on clay vases, some of which portrayed a person sitting in a posture commonly associated with Kundalini. The oldest spiritual documents depicting warriors using Kundalini Yoga from this region are the four Vedas of Hinduism, dating between 1,500 and 500 BCE. In them, we can find hymns praising soma, believing it to be a source of immortality and knowledge. In certain depictions of Lord Shiva, the crescent moon on his forehead represents soma, which is meant to stress the blissful state of radiance in the brain, only present when Kundalini is mastered.

Lord Shiva himself is thought to be the very first teacher of the Kundalini, based on Kashmir Shaivism. Shiva's three-pronged trident acts as a representation of the three aspects of mystical knowledge that he promoted. The first is abheda, or the existence without differentiation. The second one is bhedabheda, the existence with and without differentiation. And the last is bheda, or the existence as a differentiated being. These three states of the experience of consciousness are described in scriptural texts, such as the Tantras Bhairava, Rudra Tantras, and the Shiva Tantras. In Hinduism, the most explored way to awaken Kundalini is by the use of Tantras. These are various practices involving sexual arousal and are linked to a human being's ability to consciously convert these essences into the desired outcome in the brain instead of expressing them. Essentially this meant that a person who successfully awakened Kundalini is given the ability of control over their own fertility.

According to a general concept developed by historians studying Eastern cultures, Kundalini is based on Yoga Sutras. Patanjali was a sage who lived in India in the 2nd century BCE, and he developed a system of Yoga practices (also known as the eight-limbed system) that provide us with systematic guiding principles for obtaining a higher state of consciousness. Besides the complete moral and physical guide, it also teaches how to merge one's consciousness to that of deities. Another philosophy was Kashmir Shaivism that arose in the region of Kashmir, known as modern-day Pakistan today. Here, Lord Shiva appeared as Srikanth Ananth to share the sacred knowledge of achieving a blissful state of a higher power that was lost during the time of darkness (Kali Yuga).

Some sacred Hindu texts, such as the Upanishads, describe Kundalini as a form of enlightenment. The Yoga-Kundalini Upanishad is a short guide on how to awaken the Kundalini. It promotes and unites Kundalini concepts and other methods that, much like other Yoga teachings, are thought to be practiced and transmitted orally before they were codified in Patanjali's yoga sutras in 200 CE. The Yoga Upanishads were recorded much later, around 800-1800 CE. According to the latter, Kundalini practitioners were first influenced by specifically two branches of yoga; Hatha yoga and Mantra yoga. The Kundalini Yoga Upanishad was one of the texts whose teachings were founded and reformulated by various yoga traditions incorporating other methods such as Hatha yoga, Tantra, Advaita Vedanta, and the Siddha Yoga teachings of Gorakhnath originating from the 11th Century.

Egyptian Civilization

Although the written record dates Kundalini yoga to have emerged much later, it's possible that the practice of Kundalini existed in ancient Egypt for the same stretch of time as it did in the Indus valley. A similar depiction of deities from both cultures serves to prove this hypothesis. For example, Isis, the mother-goddess from Ancient Egypt, bears a huge resemblance to Shakti from India. Both goddesses were believed to have the power of resurrection or rebirth, a term used even today for the physical and spiritual transformation of someone awakened by Kundalini. Like Lord Shiva's crescent moon, Isis is almost always portrayed with a solar orb between two horns above her head. Her husband Osiris is depicted holding a curved rod, presumed by some historians to represent the spine. This could strongly indicate the extensive use of Kundalini by the ancient Egyptians. Although not part of Egyptian mythology, another unmistakable symbol of Kundalini originating from this era and is the staff of Hermes, which is still used to this day as an icon of medical practice is. It is technically of Greek origins, but given that Egypt was heavily influenced by the Roman-Greek Empire at the time, it's not strange that this symbol made its way into Egyptian lore.

The main difference between the interpretation of Kundalini in the Ancient Egyptian and Indus Valley civilizations is the focus of the practice. While the Indian culture focused more on transcendence and their standing in the afterlife, the Egyptians were more interested in developing mystical abilities. According to ancient Egyptian beliefs, Kundalini was able to bestow a powerful allure and enhance one's ability to rule over others. This is not surprising as the Egyptian civilization was more power-centric in general. There is proof that they even resorted to transferring the belief of awakening Kundalini toward the practices of alchemy and other magical abilities as well. The popular belief is that the purpose of alchemy was the conversion of metals, such as sulfur, salt and mercury, into gold. More gold meant more power, and even though financial gain was a goal in the Egyptian Kundalini-type practice, alchemy also served a higher purpose. Even magic was believed to be restricted by the Kundalini teachings. These teachings, though, condemn the use of magic for personal gain.

The Chinese Concept

The Chinese concept of chi is almost the same as that of prana when it comes to the Indian Kundalini tradition. Chi can also be regarded as being the essence of a person, and comparably to Kundalini, chi is credited for its connection with health and vitality. Similarly, when practicing Kundalini Yoga, chi can also be directed and circulated throughout the body. According to ancient Chinese traditions, this is done via practices such as chi kung and acupuncture. The meridian systems, a collection of concepts in Chinese medicine, also bear a remarkable resemblance to the energy channels used in the Indian tradition. The role of the backward flowing method, or as the Chinese called it, the reversal of the reproductive system, plays an important role in the Chinese Kundalini sphere of knowledge. As depicted in The Secret of the Golden Flower, this can be a key to getting pregnant. This indicates that the Chinese were also aware of the importance of Kundalini awakening in achieving fertility.

Other Traditions

Albeit in a veiled fashion, there are references to Kundalini present in the Judeo-Christian Tradition as well. Both the Old and New Testaments mention it in some form. The concept of Kundalini in these religious texts is believed to have been embodied as the serpent in certain instances, a symbol that held great importance to the Indus Valley or Ancient Egyptian civilizations.

Since traditional faiths focus more on experiencing the divine power of God and not on the process of actually achieving it, it seems that, unfortunately, this is where the Kundalini references end. Based on the Kundalini teachings, these mystical traditions of faith all include the perception of a divine being or higher power who can bring a person to a state of bliss. According to this perception, it won't matter what your faith is and how you chose to follow it, as Kundalini is present in all of them, regardless.

Modern Culture

India

In the early 20th century, India was under British colonial rule. In order to gain independence from the British, the Brahmins, a member of the highest caste attainable in Hinduism, had to prove that they are able to rule themselves. To do that, they had to organize their complex traditions into a more rational, westernized version. As Hinduism was the most accepted tradition, many Vedic and Yogic sects were becoming equated with it by the British. As a way to differentiate themselves from Hinduism, the Sikh tradition of the Khalsa warriors became a well-known Sikh identity for this newly formed Sikhism. To preserve and distinguish their Sikh identity, the mainstream Sikhs distanced themselves from any influences of Hinduism, the mainstream religion at the time. They lived by the Sikh Dharma that was shared by the 10 Sikh gurus and by the Siri Guru Granth Sahib, the Living Guru, which is comprised of a collection of Holy Scriptures. As their names literally mean "seeker", the Sikhs were open to all, unlike Hinduism. Kundalini yoga was one of the traditions passed on by the 4th guru of the Sikhs and was practiced in secrecy throughout India. Kundalini was mostly practiced among The Udasi's and Nirmala's (two Sikh sects), alongside many other Sikh philosophies, practices, and knowledge passed on from the remaining Sikh Gurus. During the colonial war, followers of the Udasi sect were excluded from the Pure Sikhs as a result of their remaining link to Hinduism. Due to this, all practices associated with the Udasis, such as the Kundalini Yoga, were also excluded from the mainstream Sikh practice as a final step to completely distance themselves from Hinduism. But, these teachings still continue to exist among some of the marginalized Sikh practitioners, one of them being Yogi Bhajan himself.

Western Culture

Although the healing properties of Kundalini were researched and studied by renowned psychiatrist Carl G. Jung in 1932, the actual practice of Kundalini was rarely seen in the West until the early 70s. The only other notable person who proposed a Kundalini-like concept was Wilhelm Reich. He was an American psychiatrist who theorized the existence of bio-plasma in the body called orgone. According to him, orgone was linked to oxygen. And it could be found in every cell of the human body, just like how Kundalini energy flows through the body.

Kundalini was first introduced into modern Western culture in the United States by an Indian man named Harbhajan Singh Khalsa, better known as Yogi Bhajan by Kundalini yoga practitioners. In 1969, he was also the first man who began to teach this knowledge publicly, which was a remarkable feat as it was only practiced or passed on in secrecy, even in the East. Bhajan himself was taught Kundalini in secrecy in India and had mastered the teachings by the age of 16. He was able to do this only because he was fortunate enough to be born into a wealthy family. As such, they belonged to an elite society that was privileged enough to have access to this type of teaching. As a son of a medical doctor, Bhajan was intrigued by the rapid developments of Western medicine. He was also curious about how to combine the knowledge of this scientific approach to medicine with the spiritual teachings of Kundalini, which is what ultimately brought him to Los Angeles, where he began his mission of educating and sharing this ancient knowledge with the world. His first attempt at this was preaching his methods to hippies seeking spirituality through drugs. Bhajan claimed that the same state could be achieved without the drugs simply by mastering Kundalini yoga. He also claimed Kundalini could help reverse the damage done by the drugs to the user's nervous system.

Bhajan not only predicted the current information overload brought on by 21st-century technology, but he also offered an effective method to fight the negative effects on the human nervous system. He understood that these devices were meant to help the human brain sort information, but he also knew that the flood of information would overtax our nervous system. Because of this, he encouraged everyone to empty their mind by letting all the menial information out and the healing flow of Kundalini energy in. Bhajan said that many of the stress-related and psychological illnesses are actually a symptom of a lack of inner balance and proposed Kundalini yoga as a way to effectively remedy them. According to him, in many cases, meditation and various Kundalini techniques can be much more helpful than modern Western medicine. Bhajan emphasized that instead of just numbing ourselves with drugs, yoga can help calm the nervous system effectively, preventing depression, violence, and the need for heavy medications.

Bhajan formed an ashram community of roughly 140 members in Phoenix. This local community of yogis practiced under the leadership of Bhajan until he passed away in 2004. Yogi Bhajan himself taught Kundalini Yoga and White Tantric Yoga, all around the world, until the day he died. The practices of Kundalini have evolved over time through the influence of different streams of thought and perception, changes that came before and after Yogi Bhajan. Although we know Kundalini Yoga, only as he taught it, he also studied Yoga under many teachers, all with their own diverse traditions. This way, he was able to collect and impart a combined knowledge from lots of different versions of Kundalini. He successfully grew a community of yogis who also carried on his teachings. This community continued to expand and is still innovating its teachings to this day. They made these classical yogic systems widely accessible and made sure they are applicable to the needs of modern generations. Even now, fifty years in the making, Yogi Bhajan's community of teachers still continues to change Kundalini Yoga along with the times so that we get to have an even better awakening experience today.

In modern times, Kundalini Yoga classes have moved into more traditional yoga studios. Yogi Bhajan's version of Kundalini Yoga has continued to grow its influence and quickly become popular in the Americas. Later this popularity spread to Europe, South Africa, and Australia as well. In modern times, Kundalini yoga classes have moved into more traditional yoga studios and are taught by thousands of yogis worldwide. Today's yogis, including Bhajan's former students, explain Kundalini energy to be unique to each person, similar to our DNA. They also call it a nerve of our soul, explaining the importance of connecting our nervous system to our spiritual energy.

Nowadays, Kundalini Yoga is a complex entity comprised of many different traditions that were present throughout history. From the ancient mysticality and craving for divine power, Kundalini developed over time as a science of the body. In its modern concept, the kriyas and meditations in Kundalini Yoga are designed to raise awareness of our body's function. It teaches us how to prepare the whole body, and most importantly, the nervous system, to handle the energy of Kundalini awakening. Besides the nervous system, Kundalini Yoga practices also focus on the role of the balance of the endocrine system on the body's vitality and overall well-being. All the physical yoga postures depicted in the ancient symbolic texts are still used today to activate the navel and spine chakras, as well as pressurize the energy points. In modern practices, the flow of Kundalini energy is achieved via breath work (pranayama) and the application of yogic locks of energy (bandhas). The ultimate purpose of modern Kundalini Yoga is to prepare the energy system of a human being to hold the power of the awakening. The idea here is that later an awakened body will merge its consciousness directly with the consciousness of God.

Although there is still ongoing scientific research on the benefits of Kundalini Yoga meditations and practices, following Yogi Bhajan's advice, Kundalini has been linked to successfully healing addictions and disorders such as PTSD and underlying trauma. With the help of yogic teachers, who are collecting information from the thousands of Kundalini Yoga kriyas and meditations, medical practitioners are able to apply yoga therapy in lieu of heavy medications. Despite this, there is still a lot of knowledge to be uncovered on Kundalini Yoga's roots, techniques, and possible benefits. Even the history of Yogi Bhajan's own study of Kundalini and other yoga practices is still not fully known as of today. This is why yogis around the world from diverse communities with specialized focuses and practices are still specializing and combining their expertise with the knowledge of scientists from many countries in hopes to create a complete healing practice accessible to all.

Chapter 4: Kundalini and the Ego

"Kundalini is another name for Atma, or Self or Shakti. We talk of it as being inside the body because we conceive ourselves as limited to the body. But it is in reality both inside and outside, being no other than the self, or Shakti." - Sri Ramana Maharshi

In studying Kundalini and the modes of spiritual awakening as taught in western and eastern cultures, two significant concepts are discussed extensively in both schools of philosophy—the dissolution of the ego and the energetic awakening of Kundalini. Both these things simultaneously exist and are innately connected to each other. The concept of Kundalini comes from the early teachings of Hinduism. It is described as a form of intrinsic energy that is stored at the base of the spine. The power of Kundalini can be awakened through tantric practice, which ultimately leads to spiritual liberation. The concept of the ego, on the other hand, comes from a Western school of teaching. Renowned psychologist Sigmund Freud described the ego as part of the human psyche, which works as a mediator between the id and superego, helping humans be more rational and functional beings. In modern English, the word ego has a broader meaning, which refers to self-esteem and the conscious thinking of the "self" within us.

While the existence of the ego and Kundalini energy may appear to contrast each other at first, they actually complement each other in many ways. However, in the end, it is the death of the ego that enables one to complete the full awakening of their Kundalini energy.

The Death of the Ego

Death or the permanent end of something is often associated with darkness and mourning. We spend our entire lives evading the possibility of death yet are always denied physical immortality, as everyone inevitably has to face someday. The death of the ego, however, should be considered cause for celebration. It is positive, enlightening, illuminating, and beautiful. It is the ultimate and pivotal part of the spiritual awakening journey that is essential to unleashing the ultimate power of Kundalini energy. In Kundalini teachings, it is said that the death of the ego happens in the blink of an eye. However, making it to the complete and eternal cessation of the ego and the full awakening of the Kundalini energy happens to be a rather drawn-out process that comes in gradual stages that requires an immense amount of patience.

The ego is the sense of self that a sentient being has, giving them the ability to feel and experience the process of living, rather than being a passive participant in life. It is the ego that allows us to feel emotions like happiness, joy, and gratitude, however also pain, suffering, and grief. The concept of the ego is presented and criticized in almost all different spiritual teachings, connecting it largely with suffering. Even the seemingly positive feelings created by the ego, such as love and kindness, tend to eventually lead to suffering. For example, when you love someone deeply, and they do not reciprocate the feeling, it brings you pain that you do not have control over. If you are unconditionally kind to someone, and they disappoint you or betray your trust and kindness, that also leads to sadness and suffering. These kinds of negative emotions and the energy they emit tend to obstruct the full attaining of Kundalini energy.

The Dual Nature of the Ego

As previously mentioned, one of the most common metaphors used to describe Kundalini energy is that it is like a "coiled snake" that rests at the bottom of your spine, filled with power and potential, but hindered by the negative power of the ego. It can be awakened even with the presence of the ego, but in order to attain Kundalini's full potential, the ego should be eliminated fully. Unlike the Kundalini energy, the human ego adheres to duality. It means dividing the forces of life into two different categories—good and bad, love and hate, right and wrong. The reality of Kundalini is that they cannot be divided as such. There is no inherent right and wrong in the world. The awakening of the Kundalini energy needs the acceptance of reality in order to unleash its full potential. Duality of the ego leads to suffering and breeds many hindering emotions, such as hatred, alienation, and judgment.

Kundalini energy, however, requires the unconditional acceptance of the wholeness of life. There are no unacceptable or unexpected people or experiences. Every person, belief, thought, and experience should be embraced as one receives them, without restricting either one in dual categories. Kundalini energy can be awakened by many different methods, including meditation, breathing, and tantric practices. Each of these methods requires reducing or suppressing the ego. For example, meditation requires focused attention and a heightened state of awareness, which cannot be attained when the ego is responsible for distracting the mind. This is why the death of the ego is essential for fully awakening the Kundalini energy.

Throughout history, one can deduce that most of human suffering and chaos were and still are, caused by people who live their lives guided by their egos. Mental illness is rampant, with even the youngest minds being prone to depression and chronic anxiety. There is hatred and jealousy everywhere. On a global level, there is poverty, war, and destruction of the environment that we live in. All of this chaos is, ultimately, a reflection of the ego-based lives that we live. Within such a setting, it can be extremely difficult to awaken the energy of Kundalini that is resting within every one of us. Everyone suffers because most people are convinced that they are isolated in this larger universe, a feeling which can be attributed to our egos. In Kundalini, every being, living or otherwise, is connected through a universal web of energy, creating a larger consciousness that transcends trivial emotions such as rage and melancholy.

The death of the ego is metaphorical and does not signify death in the sense of morbid destruction. The "death" of the ego is about slowly diminishing the power that it has on a person's mind, finally rendering it completely powerless. When the power of the ego diminishes, it makes it easier for the mind to remove the lens of duality through which it was used to look at the world. The complete removal of the ego feeds the coiled snake of Kundalini energy that resides within us, allowing it to be all-embracing and powerful. Ideally, awakened Kundalini energy improves a person's intuition, brainpower, willpower, and creativity in a way that is difficult to fathom by a mind that is controlled by the ego.

The Gradual Path Towards the Dissolution of Ego in the Journey to Awaken Kundalini Energy

"When you come to the ultimate experience in meditation when you come to your deepest core, you are no one. You are a vast emptiness. You can become afraid in meditation because the deeper you go in meditation, the more you realize that you are nobody, a nothingness. It is a death of the ego." — Swami Dhyan Giten

The dissolution of your ego is less about destroying something and more about returning to a pure state we were born in, which also showcases who you really are. However, while the final result of freeing yourself fully of your ego can feel incredibly wonderful and beautiful, the process that leads up to it can feel horrific in many ways, especially for those who have not previously taken up a spiritual journey. It is, therefore, important to always remember the divine relief and the power that awaits at the end of the path as one takes gradual steps towards the death or dissolution of the ego.

Spiritual Awakening

This is the moment when you essentially "wake up" and come to the realization that your potential is higher than the triviality of day-to-day life. You wake up to life as if you have been trapped in a long slumber, even though you have lived on this earth for many years. This realization that there is a larger spiritual path ahead of you comes to different people in different ways. It could be a sudden existential crisis as a young college student, an unexpected tragedy that befalls you or your loved ones, a terminal illness that reduces your life to a few numbers, or even completely out of the blue. You could simply wake up one day and ask yourself questions such as "what is the purpose of life?"

"The Dark Night of the Soul"

The "Dark Night of the Soul" describes the phase directly after one's awakening from reality and the onset of a strong feeling of disillusionment with your life and everything in it. It is a soul-crushing experience that can feel dark and depressing, but it is essential for the process of fully disconnecting oneself from one's ego. This stage may feel lonely and even scary at times. It is natural to feel completely lost and to experience the true pain of everything that was ignored for so long. It is during "The Dark Night of the Soul" that eliminates the need for one's ego, which is responsible for a person's clinging to material things. This stage may bring many emotions to the surface, which are integral to reach a state of catharsis.

Spiritual Seeking

Once the spiritual seeking and the "The Dark Night of the Soul" pass, the next stage brings on a massive thirst for knowledge. It is quite likely that many readers of this book are already in this particular stage of their journey towards spiritual awakening. Usually, it can take several attempts of seeking knowledge in various places and disciplines to finally come upon the power of Kundalini energy. Pursuing spiritual disciplines and fields such as yoga, zen teachings, astrology, and Reiki are some of the most popular spiritual seeking paths people come across in this state of spiritual seeking. After a stressful period of catharsis, this state is exciting and invigorating. It can take months or even years of experimenting with different spiritual practices until one day the dedicated spiritual seeker finds the power of Kundalini energy.

"Satori"

There is a teaching in Zen Buddhism called "satori", which translates to momentary enlightenment. This is a defining moment in the process of ego dissolution. Satori is having a clear but small glimpse of a potentially attainable higher consciousness. At that moment, your ego is completely silenced, and you momentarily experience the divine freedom that you are tirelessly seeking. It is a force that helps you see the process through to the very end, now that you have experienced the state that you have only read or heard about. For some people, the moment of "satori" can feel exhilarating, but for others it may feel scary or intimidating. Therefore, at this stage, it is to have a teacher or trusted practitioner to guide you through the process. It is extremely important to be guided correctly through the process, as your spiritual growth can stagnate at this point.

The Elder Soul

Once you experience "satori" and feel compelled to push yourself deeper down the path towards awakening, you will start developing a certain spiritual discernment. Thanks to the kriyas you've been adhering to, you are now familiar with your mind and body, and you are aware of the way spiritual energy affects you. You have seen pain and suffering, you have extensively studied different paths to spiritual freedom, and you are now armed with the absolute knowledge that in order to stop your suffering, you have to achieve complete death or dissolution of the ego. At this stage, you can easily connect to a higher self, having experienced minimal success, and self-discipline comes to you without having to put too much effort into it. You are patient, you are focused, and you have a calm and matured soul. You can almost see the end of the path at this point.

The Deconstruction

This is a stage of surrender and letting go. It involves gently removing all the destructive behavior patterns and limiting beliefs you have in your life. You are able to fully disconnect yourself from the many attachments created by your ego. Your mind is neutral; it does not hold intense emotions, such as hatred or obsession. You are filled with grace, trust, and humility. You feel content and completely at peace with yourself and the universe around you.

The End of Search

You have come to a stop. You have a deep and absolute understanding of all that you are, all that you need, and all that you will be. At this stage, the sense of perpetual exhilaration you feel is not connected to any kind of need to be something, lose something or accomplish something. You see through all the illusions your ego has created that, so far, have masked the suffering that it always brought to your life. You are no longer relentlessly looking for love or joy outside yourself, like everyone else. Being a human, your ego still exists as a part of your mind, but it does not have control or any hold on you. You no longer perceive the world through a lens of duality. You are at peace.

The Awakening of Kundalini

As previously established, the first step to awakening Kundalini energy is by freeing yourself from the negative power of ego. By now, you understand that the ability to awaken this energy is inherent in every single one of us. Kundalini energy has been within us since our birth, inherited and empowered by the feminine power and love of our mother, father, and numerous ancestors who passed down their wisdom to us. Some people are naturally more in tune with their inner selves, while others may need time to suppress the power of ego that has been controlling them their entire lives. Ego is all that they have known, and to let go of it can feel extremely vulnerable and painful at first. Once a person completes the stage of fully letting go of their ego, they find the ultimate power of Kundalini waiting for them on the other end.

Think about Kundalini as a soft ember that has been hidden within you all along. Without the means of flourishing, the roaring fire is due to constant suppression that comes from the massive ego that obstructs any possibility of instigating that fire within you. Kundalini energy is a fire that is within. While it may feel abstract and insignificant when the ego is too inflated, once it is fully activated and the ego has been diminished, it becomes a massive fire of power, creativity, and energy that cannot be easily restricted. Once Kundalini energy is activated and the ego perishes, the serpent-like Kundalini energy flows throughout the body and the mind, nourishing all the chakras in the body with positive energy.

Another important thing to remember when speaking of Kundalini energy and ego is that there are two contrasting ways to awaken the sacred energy within. The "snake" can actually be awakened both peacefully and creatively with a diminished ego and a drive for all the good things in the world, and also rather destructively and driven by the ego. Just like fire, the raw energy that is inside each of us can be used for progress and destruction. A person who is striving to awaken Kundalini energy as a way of enhancing their spirituality and the power of the mind should always do so following pure and virtuous methods, similar to those discussed earlier

The Connection between the Ego and Unleashing the Power of Kundalini

"When the sleeping goddess Kundalini is awakened through the grace of the teacher, then all the subtle lotuses and worldly bonds are readily pierced through and through. Let the wise person forcibly and firmly draw up the goddess Kundalini, for She is the giver of all miraculous powers." - Shiva Samhita

The power of Kundalini rests at the bottom of the spine until you work towards awakening it and diminishing your ego enough to harness that power. The goal of every practice towards tapping that coiled snake is to get it to wake up and spread its power all the way towards the head, symbolizing the connection between brain and psyche. From the root chakra closer to the place where Kundalini power originates from, passing the sacral, solar plexus, heart, throat, and finally, the third eye chakra that controls imagination and wisdom towards the ultimate crown chakra that controls your spiritual connections, Kundalini energy activates your entire being and makes you the best version of yourself. If there's one thing that keeps obstructing this healing path, it is your overwhelming ego and the many emotional upheavals that come with it.

Once we do that, we are able to merge with the universe and the pure consciousness of the cosmic presence that surrounds us from the moment we are born to the moment we die. The awakening of your Kundalini energy and the dissolution of your ego is both the path and the goal of your spiritual journey to unlock a higher level of consciousness. The much sought-after effects of this journey include having a high level of contentment, clarity, and creativity.

Just like any two powerful yet contrasting forces such as love and hatred, the connection between Kundalini energy and the ego can be destructive at times. At its purest level, without any kind of tainting through the ego, Kundalini energy comes off as pure creative power. However, when channeled through paths, like sexuality and methods that are influenced by the ego, it can easily turn into a dangerous force. Just like certain kinds of snake venom that can either heal or aggravate one's condition, Kundalini energy can empower us or hold us hostage. This duality, however, only presents itself if the ego is still present. The dual-lens through which the ego perceives the world results in the pure power of the Kundalini energy being tainted. Therefore, working towards a complete dissolution of the ego is essential in the path to awakening Kundalini and harnessing its full potential.

Earlier in this chapter, it was mentioned how the death or the dissolution of the ego is a gradual process. The awakening of Kundalini, however, does not happen gradually. It is not like one day you have a little Kundalini, and the next day it gradually increases. The full awakening of the coiled snake that rests within you is a massive quantum leap of pure awareness. As you work on your meditation and other tantric practices, and you might feel a little spark of energy every now and then, it is quite likely that it is not Kundalini energy. Our body is a magical vessel for all kinds of amazing energies given to us by the universe. In times, these milder spiritual energies get awakened simply because your body is starting to create the spiritual environment that is needed for the Kundalini energy to rise. These energies show that your mind is gradually diminishing the power of your ego and carefully preparing the way for an astronomical rise of Kundalini energy that will happen in the near future.

As humans, our brains constantly crave gratification. It is the reason that we are easily distracted by trivial things, and it is often hard to focus on a complex path that takes us to a higher state of being. Unsurprisingly, it is our ego that craves instant gratification. This means that as you walk the path of dissolving your ego, you may start telling yourself that you feel tiny bursts of Kundalini energy within you. It feeds our pride and often makes us feel superior to those who are around us. Our ego slows down any progress we are making towards awakening the energy within us. It is for that reason you need to first focus on controlling and diminishing the power that your ego has on you. The moment you embark on the path to awakening Kundalini's energy by pleasing your ego and gaining validation from people around you is the moment you sabotage your own journey.

Awakening the power of Kundalini is a purely selfless act. The more you feed your sense of self and pursue pleasure and status, the more you are suppressing the magical energy residing within you that can potentially elevate your entire being to levels that you cannot even comprehend. Your ego is the biggest obstruction to any kind of spiritual practice that you strive to follow. Working towards awakening your Kundalini without humbling your ego can lead you to much suffering. Therefore, you should always clear your path towards spirituality by shedding your ego and fully dissolving its hold on you.

> *"Before awakening the Kundalini, you must have deha suddhi (purity of body), nadi suddhi (purity of the nadis), manas suddhi (purity of mind), and buddhi suddhi (purity of the intellect)."* - Swami Sivanand

Chapter 5: Benefits of Kundalini

Kundalini, derived from the Sanskrit word "kundal", meaning coiled up like a snake, refers to the spiritual energy that rests at the base of the spine, like a serpent, within our body. Practicing Kundalini yoga activates this dormant energy. The process of activating the Kundalini energy, also known as shakti, present in our bodies is also known as Kundalini awakening. Also referred to as the Yoga of Awareness, Kundalini awakening enriches the practitioner's perception of life by making them more aware of their inner-self and the outside world as well.

Practitioners of Kundalini yoga believe that there are seven energy centers, or chakras, in our body. Starting from the root, the chakras move up the spine through the sacrum, solar plexus, heart, throat, third eye to finally reach the crown. Out of the seven chakras, six are located within the physical body, while the seventh is located outside of us, right above our heads. Through the practice of Kundalini yoga, the seven chakras can be roused effectively.

From strengthening your consciousness to spiritual enlightenment, Kundalini yoga is believed to alter the practitioner's life in dramatic ways. People who practice Kundalini yoga experience lower anxiety levels and higher energy states. Many science-backed research papers reveal the limitless benefits of practicing Kundalini yoga. In this chapter, we'll underline the key transformations that people experience by practicing Kundalini yoga.

Amplifies Energy

Kundalini yoga is essentially the combination of meditation, yoga poses, breath control, and chanting of mantras (spiritual phrases). A session of Kundalini yoga starts with deep breathing and simple warm-up exercises for the spinal cord. This is done to essentially make the body more receptive to the unrealized energy present within it. As we proceed, a blend of specific breathing techniques and physical poses help transfer the energy upwards, from one energy chakra to the next. Each of the seven energy centers in our body is opened through the performing of specific poses, or asanas, combined with chanting or systematic breathing.

Performing Kundalini yoga empowers an individual with radiant energy. Also known as kriyas, a specific set of exercises are performed to remove any blockages in our body. Performing these kriyas helps generate energy in the practitioner's body, makes them calm, and silences the mind's chatter while completely relaxing the physical body.

The chanting of mantras reverberates powerful vibrations throughout the body. When kriyas and mantras combine, they amplify the energy felt by the yogi or practitioner. As the level of energy rises, the chakras are activated sequentially. When the final chakra is activated, the energy level of a yogi is at its fullest. With consistent practice, the high-energy states tend to last longer and take a permanent form.

Boosts Body Positivity

The exercises required to be performed for Kundalini yoga can be challenging. However, even with little practice, one can sense the flow of positivity in their life. Kundalini yoga rejuvenates our entire body on a cellular level. The different types of asanas and breathing techniques can strengthen the core of the body. They also have a positive effect on the endocrine and nervous systems. Regular practice of Kundalini yoga can help you keep many diseases from afflicting you. Gradually, confidence and a sense of self-care build up within the body, changing your perception of your physical self.

Yoga poses like backbends, crunches, downward dog position, and leg lifts aim at improving your posture and the strength of core muscles in your body. Performing vigorous yoga exercises will positively affect your physical as well as mental state. The different breathing exercises involved in Kundalini yoga require the practitioner to control the abdominal muscles, strengthening them more over time. If you regularly practice the kriyas, you'll avoid countless abdomen-related problems like cramping, irritation, abdominal pain, and other diseases.

Once you start performing Kundalini yoga perfectly, you'll start beaming with positive energy. Over time, your willpower and self-reliance will have greatly improved. You'll feel fresh, fit, and healthy at all times. The boost in body positivity will be visible not only to you but to others around you as well. You will start to appreciate yourself as you become more confident. With consistent practice of

Kundalini yoga, you'll notice a considerable improvement in the state of your mind, body, and soul.

Cognitive Improvements

The various meditation practices and techniques involved in Kundalini yoga can help with the treatment of mild cognitive impairments or similar disorders. According to a 2004 study published in the Journal of Complementary and Alternative Medicine, psychiatric disorders like insomnia, dyslexia, obsessive-compulsive disorder (OCD), substance abuse disorders, phobias, and other major depressive disorders can be treated by Kundalini yoga.

In a 2007 study published in International Psychogeriatrics, a randomized controlled trial of 81 participants was held to recognize the effectiveness of Kundalini yoga on mild cognitive impairment. The participants were randomly divided into two groups. People in one group practiced Kundalini yoga, while people in the second group underwent memory enhancement training. Both groups showed improvement in memory functioning, but only the people from the Kundalini yoga group showed improvement in cognitive skills like problem-solving and reasoning.

The study also established that practicing this form of yoga can help improve cognitive functioning, enhance your memory functioning, and help deal with moods such as apathy, resilience, and depression.

Practicing Kundalini yoga helps the practitioners delve deep within themselves and explore their inner being on another level. Backed by science and various researches, practicing

Kundalini yoga is an effective way to treat sleeping and other psychiatric disorders. It can dramatically improve your mental well-being. That being said, it also helps people improve their level of self-awareness, which further improves their mental clarity and problem-solving skills. If you regularly practice Kundalini yoga, you'll experience increased productivity and effectiveness in everything that you do.

Enlightens Spiritually

Kundalini yoga has the power to transcend the yogi and help them connect to the eternal source of all energies; the universe. The word "transcend" itself means "to rise". Concerning Kundalini yoga, the yogi elevates the chakras in their body to reach the highest energy level, which leads to full synchronization with the universe's energies. According to Sadhguru, the founder of Isha Foundation in India, when the yogi is in unison with the universe, they are all-seeing and all-knowing. It means that when you're deep in Kundalini meditation, all your thoughts are dialed down, and you develop a more intimate connection with yourself and the others around you through a spiritual plain.

Through the practice of Kundalini yoga, you connect with the universe on a deeper level. It is common for Kundalini yoga practitioners to give up on habits that are harmful to themselves and the world. Habits like smoking, drinking, and drugs can be easily shunned because Kundalini yoga gives a more effective "high" than any external substance ever can. It becomes easier to leave behind the pain of the past and forget about the uncertainty of the future.

Kundalini yoga brings your consciousness to the present moment and helps you hold on to the beautiful experience of being "one with nature". Being immersed in the experience of Kundalini yoga can open up pathways for you to connect yourself with the divine power of the universe. The people who are successful in awakening their Kundalini find bliss in every moment and have a truly spiritual experience.

Enriches Empathy

Practitioners believe that every chakra in the body serves a purpose. By activating the heart chakra, the yogi can open their heart to the world and spread the endless love that they experience within themselves. By feeling the endless energy flowing within themselves, practitioners of Kundalini yoga can relate to the outside world on a spiritual level. Practicing Kundalini yoga can fill you with kindness and gratitude. Kundalini yoga transforms the nature of a practitioner to be compassionate, forgiving, and empathetic.

By activating the throat chakra, the yogi can openly express themselves to the world with tenderness and gentleness. Kundalini yoga strengthens the power of the conscious mind and develops the power of intuition. When you're deep into a meditative state, you'll find all the answers you're looking for. As you practice more and more, your feelings and thoughts align themselves to help silence the chatter of the mind and focus on the gut feeling.

As you start understanding life on a deeper level, you become empathetic to everything that crosses your path. It becomes natural to connect with all forms of life, be it another human being or an animal. Many practitioners believe that practicing Kundalini yoga helps you realize psychic abilities and mystical powers. Awakening the Kundalini can open up multiple dimensions of your being, and with proper utilization, it can alter your life forever.

Improves Charisma

A person with an awakened Kundalini may experience a boost in confidence as well as willpower. A person like this can experience bliss at an extreme level. With the increase in self-reliance and self-love, the enlightened individual will appear to be very charismatic and be in possession of a fascinating character. Kundalini yoga can make the yogi radiate tremendous energy that presents itself through a silver aura encompassing them. Masters of Kundalini yoga exercise a mesmerizing charm that often inspires devotion in others.

When all the seven chakras of the Kundalini are activated, the energy awakens the yogi to a world of mystical wonder. It is common for the practitioners of Kundalini yoga to brush with impressive experiences like clairvoyance and out-of-body experiences. In the state of meditative absorption, a yogi can experience interesting phenomena, like hearing the sound of quiet humming, distant chirping, or music. Those who experience the deepest levels usually having stronger sensitivity, increased energy levels, and more charisma.

Increases Creativity

The kriyas, asanas, and breathing techniques involved in practicing Kundalini yoga help improve balance, enhance stability, and increase creativity. Usually, the right hemisphere of your brain, which is essentially responsible for creativity, is less stimulated than the left. This is because we spend more time thinking, analyzing, or worrying about things. With systemic movements, rhythmic chanting, and controlled breathing, the left and right hemisphere of our brain are equally stimulated, as these practices engage both. When the logical and the creative part of your mind are equally balanced, you'll find yourself more inclined towards a specific form of art like dancing, singing, or writing.

Practicing Kundalini yoga removes all the accumulated emotions, thoughts, and worries from our bodies. Being free of all the things that weigh you down, the infinite possibilities offered by life start to come into view. Kundalini can increase the amount of time you spend on creative and productive things. It makes us realize our path and the reason for our very existence, making us feel the need to pursue the things were are passionate about with determination. It is an experience that can only be witnessed, not expressed.

Inner Peace

Kundalini yoga is known to cleanse the participant's nervous system and establish a balance in the hormonal glands. That said, practicing Kundalini yoga can help remove mental blockages and resolve negative behavioral patterns such as addictions, fear, and insecurities. The purifying energy obtained from Kundalini yoga gives you greater strength and the ability to have control over how you react to certain situations in life.

The balance between the negative and the positive energy in our body gives rise to a neutral state that helps a person act without being made to feel biased or manipulated by emotions. Kundalini yoga helps the participants to train their minds to be more patient and less reactive to external factors. Not being reactive does not mean suppressing your emotions. It means the yogi develops a deeper understanding and awareness that helps them act in a way to produce the best possible outcome.

The neutral state of mind brings immense peace because nothing can bother the calmness that comes after practicing Kundalini yoga. Kundalini empowers the individual to make decisions from a state of non-attachment. So ultimately, the yogi is detached from all external distractions and finds himself in a peaceful state of mind.

Makes you Mindful

One of the most important benefits of Kundalini yoga is that it helps the yogi live their life with utmost mindfulness. Once you start believing in the magic of the eternal universe, you become more mindful, and all of your actions are more intentional. You become aware of the consequences of every move that you make. Masters of yoga believe that practicing Kundalini yoga can free you from the cycle of karma as if the universe lets go of your past actions. They believe that positive intentions, combined with real effort, can burn off your past deeds. Kundalini yoga helps people walk the path of mindful living to become receptive to the infinite possibilities of life.

Relieves Stress and Anxiety

All participants of Kundalini yoga experience a steady drop in stress and anxiety levels, making it an effective tool to battle anxiety disorders. The various asanas and kriyas help attain a state of deep relaxation that enables healing of the body. Practicing Kundalini yoga regularly can make you flexible and more resilient to face everyday stress with ease. It helps in dealing with the negative effects of stress and anxiety effectively.

In a research paper published in the International Journal of Yoga, it has been noted that the regular practice of Kundalini yoga can significantly reduce the level of the cortisol hormones, also known as stress hormones, in the participant's body. The alpha waves present in our bodies are neutral oscillations that reduce the stress hormones in our bodies. Practicing Kundalini yoga can increase the activity level of the alpha waves in our body and decrease the rate of respiration. This is how Kundalini yoga helps the body to calm down and make positive changes in behavior and how your body presents itself.

Strengthens Body & Mind

The exercises and poses involved in Kundalini yoga are difficult and strenuous to perform. There is rarely any rest period between two physical postures or activities. The difficult and challenging yoga poses condition the bodies and minds of the participants to be patient and resilient, while it also strengthens their physical bodies. The meditative state induced by performing Kundalini yoga can help bring mental clarity and a positive outlook towards life. A healthy mindset and a healthy body can make the experience of life all the more fruitful. Kundalini yoga can make you physically strong and mentally sharp.

Treats Addictions

Kundalini yoga is known to be an effective complementary treatment for addictive and compulsive behavioral patterns. Researchers believe it to be a major therapeutic aid to train the mind to prevent factors that lead to this kind of destructive behavior. Procrastination, chronic stress, resentment, and self-hatred are examples of behavior that can be treated by Kundalini yoga. Regular practice can help to successfully counteract these behaviors.

When the energy centers of the body are activated, self-awareness is increased tenfold. This can increase insights and help people cope with their addictions. The behavioral and neural processes involved in the treatment of addiction and relapse are impacted by increased self-awareness. Negative thoughts are rare to those who practice Kundalini yoga regularly.

Welcoming Well-Being

The practice of Kundalini yoga involves chanting sacred mantras. These holy chants are strong positive vibrations that have the potential to awaken the sleeping energy at the bottom of your spine. Proper pronunciation and musical chanting are known to generate vibrations and energy. The sensation almost feels like a snake crawling up on your spine. Many of the mantras chanted while practicing Kundalini yoga are proven to increase the dopamine levels in the body that are responsible for making us feel happy and content. The profound effects of Kundalini yoga include general happiness, vitality, and well-being.

Kundalini energy is believed to be divine cosmic energy that can transform a person on mental, spiritual, and physical levels. By practicing the correct form of Kundalini yoga, people can understand the multiple dimensions that comprise life. If Kundalini yoga is practiced correctly, it can change your life for the better. Here's a list of a few signs that are a result of Kundalini awakening.

- Feelings of weightlessness and floating sensations are often experienced during Kundalini yoga.

- High energy levels and vibrations passing through the spine are also commonly noticed by Kundalini yoga practitioners.

- Some of the permanent changes include spiritual awakening and transformation.

- Trance-like states of bliss and joy are often associated with Kundalini awakening.

- Visions of bright light and vague shapes are commonly reported during Kundalini yoga practices.

To summarize this chapter, here are the key takeaway points that underlined the benefits of Kundalini yoga.

- Kundalini is the dormant energy resting at the base of the spine, which, when activated, can transcend a being to other dimensions of life.

- Kundalini can help treat mental and physical illnesses and cure problems like headaches, insomnia, phobias, and anxiety.

- It helps bring mental stability, emotional balance, self-reliance and boosts a positive mindset. It also improves cognitive functioning like problem-solving and reasoning.

- Kundalini yoga can compel the participants to avoid unhealthy or harmful habits that lead to a destructive lifestyle.

- The feeling of empathy is enhanced in people who practice Kundalini yoga. They can connect to others as well as themselves on a deeper level. Often the empathy is transformed to telepathy when the participants of Kundalini yoga are completely immersed in the experience.

- Kundalini yoga can improve the participant's confidence, awareness, memory, willpower, and concentration levels.

- Attaining other spiritual skills is made possible with the help of Kundalini yoga. Positive and negative situations do not affect the way a yogi reacts to them. They stay detached and unbiased to attain the best possible result.

- Kundalini yoga brings peace, calmness, creativity, and happiness to all those who successfully activate all the energy centers in their bodies.

- It encourages people to live a mindful life that is devoid of stress and anxiety.

- Practicing Kundalini yoga can strengthen your body and mind. It can clear your subconscious and help you overcome addictive behaviors.

Chapter 6: A Guide to Chakras

As mentioned before, awakening the Kundalini requires energy, and that energy is released through the seven energy centers or chakras in the body. For the majority of individuals, these chakras remain blocked. Unblocking them can release the energy, letting it flow uninterruptedly through every organ, nerve, vessel, and cell in the body. Chakras form the passage to increase connectivity between mind, body, and soul. Kundalini Yoga is designed to unblock and balance the flow of energy in chakras. If practiced under proper guidance, you can achieve spiritual awakening, helping you live your life in a balanced way.

The 7 Chakras of Life

1. Muladhara (Root Chakra)

Element: Earth

Color: Red

Sound: Lam

Life Theme: Muladhara is the first chakra which you will find at the base of the spine. Muladhara, as the name suggests, means "Root".

Natural Element: Earth

It is associated with the earth element. It is related to the ability to dig in and find things rooted firmly in life.

The Motif of Root Chakra

It is directly associated with root issues like insecurity, basic needs, family, and relationships.

Blocked Muladhara Energy and its Physical Signs

- Weight gain
- Pelvic pain
- Constipation
- Lethargy

Blocked Muladhara Energy and Mental Signs

- Lack of attention
- Increased anxiety and fear of the unknown
- Mental exhaustion
- Stress
- Inability to take any action
- The feeling of being stuck

Benefits of Root Chakra Alignment

It improves family ties and improves survival skills. The earliest memories are stored here. When it is balanced, you feel confident, strong and you can properly take care of yourself. When it is blocked, you become needy, self-destructive, and have low self-esteem. With the proper balance of chakra, you feel great, and you can stand on your own two feet. You give importance to self-care.

Pose for this chakra - Crow Pose (Bakasana)

- You must start with a mountain pose.

- Squat and place hands down on the floor.

- Keep your hands shoulder-width apart.

- Then, slowly raise your hips, placing your knees in the triceps of the upper side of your hands.

- Move the weight onto your hands, straighten the elbows, and be in this position for 10/seconds.

- Lower the feet and back to Uttanasana.

2. Svadhisthana (Sacral or Pelvic Chakra)

Element: Water

Color: Orange

Sound: Yam

Life Theme: The second chakra is Pelvic Chakra which is associated with orange color. It is located in the inner pelvis region at the lower belly.

The Symbol of Pelvic Chakra is orange with six petals around the center. The center surrounded by petals of Lotus flower represents death, birth, and rebirth. The circles represent the connection between moon phases and creativity.

Natural Element: Water

It is associated with water, which symbolizes flexibility, flow, and freedom of emotions. It is related to fun, flexibility, and flow. Once balanced, you will feel creatively high and will improve your relationship with yourself and others. You will learn to know the depth of your feelings. You will become more expressive and interact with healthier boundaries.

The Motif of Root Chakra

This chakra is related to creativity and sensuality. It gives overall enjoyment in life. When the chakra is balanced, you will find your relationship with yourself great and pleasurable.

Blocked Muladhara Energy and Physical Signs

- Bad functioning of reproductive parts
- Kidney ailments
- Bladder ailments
- Disharmony in lower abdominal parts

Blocked Muladhara Energy and Mental Signs

- Emotional blockages
- Decreased sex drive

- Overindulgence in sexual acts

- Difficulty expressing emotions

- No creativity

- The feeling of being overwhelmed in every situation

Benefits of Pelvic Chakra alignment

Balancing the Pelvic Chakra enhances creativity, passion, pleasure, and a healthy sense of relationships. When this Chakra is aligned, you have peace of mind, and your body is full of fluidity, relaxation, and fertility.

Attaining alignment requires you to block bad habits and work in harmony to achieve a healthy body, mind, and soul. As a way to get started, you can perform various yoga poses like Malasana, Goddess Pose, Frog Pose, or Happy Baby Pose. You can also use crystals and stones to balance the chakra.

Pose for this Chakra - Frog Pose (Mandukasana)

- Kneel down on a flat surface while keeping your knees apart.

- Flex the feet to make your inner part touch the feet on the ground.

- Your ankles must not be greater than 90 degrees.

- When you are comfortable staying in this position, lower your forearms.

- Look down but keep the neck extended.

- Stay in this position for some time while taking deep breaths.

3. Manipura (Navel Chakra)

Element: Fire

Color: Yellow

Sound: Ram

Life Theme: Manipura Chakra is also known as Navel Chakra or Solar Plexus, which means "lustrous gem of the city".

Natural Element: Fire

It is related to fire and represents a sense of self. The color yellow is associated with it, which is the color of the sun.

The Motif of Navel Chakra

It is linked with self-esteem, personal identity, a sense of purpose, metabolism, and digestion.

Blocked Muladhara Energy and its Physical Signs

- Digestive issues
- Constipation
- Irritable bowel syndrome

- Eating disorders
- Diabetes
- Ulcers
- Liver and Colon issues
- Pancreatic issues

Blocked Muladhara Energy and Mental Signs

- Poor self-control, along with a rigid and aggressive nature
- Failure to take positive action
- Lost willingness to find individuality, power of understanding, and identification
- Quick, aggressive responses
- Feeling of demotivation

Benefits of Navel Chakra alignment

You will feel empowered and comfortable connecting with your own self and people. Upon activating this chakra, you will have a deeper insight into your life. You will achieve inner happiness, and the outer sources of happiness will not affect you.

Pose for this Chakra - Bow Pose (Dhanurasana)

- Lie down with your chest facing the floor.

- Fold the legs at the knees, raised upwards.

- Take your hands to the back and hold the feet with them, lifting the body from the chest. This makes your body resemble a bow.

- Hold this position for some time and breathe deeply and evenly.

4. Anahata (Heart Chakra)

Element: Air

Color: Green

Sound: Yam

Life Theme: It is the fourth chakra located in your heart. When it is blocked, it will have serious repercussions on your love life. It is related to forgiveness and empathy, as well as unconditional love, joy, and compassion. It is a source of profound truths and depth that you cannot express in words.

Natural Element: Air

The heart chakra is connected to the element of air. Air symbolizes love and spirituality. To embrace love, we have to keep our hearts open to let the love flow through. It is the color green that transforms energy. When the chakra is healthy, you feel love, joy, and compassion. You will feel open to any experience in life. You will see beauty and love all around.

Blocked Muladhara Energy and its Mental & Physical Signs

- Lung ailment
- Heart ailments
- Hands, arms, and chest ailments
- Bad circulation of blood
- Increase in blood pressure
- The feeling of being alone
- Isolating yourself from others
- Feeling jealous and holding grudges against people
- Not trusting anyone
- Fear of intimacy

How to Balance the Heart Chakra

Maintain a gratitude journal, perform meditation, and the energy from a rose quartz crystal to open your heart. Drink rose tea and practice heart-positive affirmation. When you stimulate this chakra, you heal the wounds of the past, learn to love and maintain a healthy relationship with those you love. When you are stuck in your heart, you will feel inner pain that you cannot see. With the help of simple tools, you can open your heart space with no grudges.

You feel heavy at heart because you keep grudges in your hearts. It makes life miserable in the long run. It gives us a dysfunctional relationship. A blocked heart chakra leads to isolation. So, practice opening your heart and feeling the beauty all around. Feel the love, and you will be blessed with beauty all around.

Pose for this Chakra - Camel Pose (Ustrasana)

- Kneel down on the floor.

- The lower leg and thighs should be at 90 degrees and move your thighs inward.

- Then bend toward the back, and your hands should touch the soles of your feet.

- Then arch the back and have your upper body face the ceiling.

- Take deep and even breaths and stay in this position for a few minutes.

5. Vishuddha (Throat Chakra)

Element: Ether

Color: Blue

Sound: Ham

Lift Theme: It is located in the throat, and it is known as Vishuddha chakra. It means purify or purification.

5th Chakra's Natural Element: Ether

It is related to ether. It is located around your throat and neck area. It has a total spiritual flow. To attain complete purification, you need to work in unison with other chakras to attain the optimal level of energy. It will increase your understanding and sensitivity. In return, you will gain deep access to the gift of upper chakra in a subtle way.

Life Motif of the Throat Chakra

This energy is associated with one's voice. It is related to your speaking ability, especially when it comes to truth, and you can express your ideas in a clear form. You will stay graceful and truthful. You will remain attuned with outer and inner vibrations.

Physical Signs of Blocked Vishuddha Energy

If there is a misalignment of the throat chakra, it can result in a sore throat, a thyroid problem, or shoulder and neck pains. You will have hearing issues. You will face jaw pain.

Mental Signs of Blocked Vishuddha Energy

When this chakra is misaligned, you do not know what to ask for or what you need. You are unable to get back to the world. It results in poor communication.

Energetic Benefits of Aligning the Throat Chakra

This chakra bridges the gap between the mind and the heart. When you have clear throat chakra, it opens you up to a chance of infinite wisdom. It will give you spiritual truths which can give you great flow. You can effectively ask for your needs, voice creative ideas, boundaries, love, and empathy.

When this chakra is blocked, you feel that you are unable to find the voice of truth. You will become talkative, and you do not listen to others. When you have an open chakra, you are stimulated. Your voice will move through space which will help you communicate your emotions in a healthy way. You will be good at listening and even honoring personal truths without any judgment.

Pose for this Chakra - Cobra Pose

Lie down with your chest on the floor. Now place the palms on the floor and slowly lift the torso with pressure on your palm. The feet must touch the ground. The hands should be perpendicular. Take normal breaths and stay in this position for some time.

6. Anja (Third-Eye Chakra)

Element: Light

Color: Indigo

Sound: OM

Life Theme: This chakra is located in the 3rd eye area. It means command.

6th Chakra's Natural Element: Light

It is related to light. It gives you the cosmic vision that illuminates everything without any prejudice, judgment, or expectations.

Life Motif of the Third Eye Chakra

It is associated with higher knowledge. There is a different aspect of sight that can be described as intuition. This chakra is above the eyes, which offers visual perception. Hindu culture is based on a visual culture where you can see clearly with the perception of correction.

Physical Signs of Blocked Ajna Energy

If there is any misalignment, then there could be problems like dizziness, headaches, and migraines. It is even known to cause vision problems.

Mental Signs of Blocked Ajna Energy

When the chakra goes out of balance, you will feel mental confusion.

Energetic Benefits of Aligning the Third Eye Chakra

When you try to stimulate Ajna chakra, you can see things in their original form without any ego clouding your vision. From that section, you can move on to the things which you value most in life. It makes life efficient.

It is even related to intuition and rules the function of other chakras. If it works properly, you can find inner wisdom. You can face challenges and make informed choices in life. When it is blocked, you will feel close-minded, you will become more cynical, and you will be attached to logic. When you work on this chakra, you open your mind to the bigger picture. You think from a different perspective of life. This wisdom is something you can achieve at the cosmic level.

Pose for this Chakra - Guru Pranam

- Sit on the back of your heels and kneel down.

- Bend to forward direction and keep your torso on your thighs.

- Keep the shins on the ground and then stretch the hands out in front of your chest, joining your palms in a prayer pose.

7. Sahasrara (Crown Chakra)

Element: Cosmic Energy

Color: Violet or White

Sound: OM

Life Theme: This is the 7th chakra which is located on the head; it symbolizes a thousand lotus petals.

7th Chakra's Natural Element: Thought

It is related to knowledge, enlightenment, spirit connection, and deep thoughts.

Life Motif of the Crown Chakra

When you work on this chakra, you work with a higher purpose in life. You also let go of personal misunderstandings.

Signs of Blocked Sahasrara Energy

When it is not aligned, you are led to confusion, being unfocused, imbalanced, and lacking connection. It even takes away your ability to perform practical functions.

Energetic Benefits of Aligning the Crown Chakra

It helps you achieve the ultimate level of consciousness. It helps you work towards enlightenment. It relates to beauty and the spiritual side. You will understand yourself and have a proper human experience. When energy is locked in the head, you will see unhappiness in everything. But, this chakra practice makes you feel far from all these negative emotions.

Pose for this Chakra - Sat Kriya

- Sit on the heels, raise the hands above the head, join hands and intertwine all fingers except the index fingers, which should remain outstretched

- Then bring the arms close to the ears and then squeeze to the naval point.

It is important to know that every chakra is important, and you cannot skip or neglect one chakra over another. The first three chakras are related to the elimination of the negative, be it physical or spiritual. The last three chakras are related to the accumulation of good energy and even regulation of its flow. The final chakra is related to balance. Therefore, you should perform this yoga for a while to attain the ultimate satisfaction both mentally and physically.

Why Balancing Chakras Is Important

Every individual has to face challenges every step of the way in life. This often causes stress, which leads to an inevitable blockage in the energy centers of the bodies. Channeling the energy centers to release unlimited energy can help improve your overall health. As a result, you will be able to take care of your physical and emotional well-being and move past these physical and mental ailments that hinder our ascending to a higher consciousness.

Balancing chakras helps you to control your mind and react positively to the world. This is an ancient practice that pushes the body's energy in a positive direction so that you can lead a meaningful and clutter-free life.

Furthermore, it gives you a systematic approach to living your life in a balanced form. The Chakras governing this process are rooted at various levels in your body. When you align them, you generate that divine energy within yourself.

Due to its immense benefits, more and more people are looking forward to awakening their Kundalini and releasing the blocked chakras in the body for harmony. Several yoga experts use this practice in yoga to experience a surplus supply of healthy energy.

Awakening Chakras

The practice revolves around posture, chanting, breathing, and consistency. One has to focus on many things before only one can achieve the ultimate target. But the entire process can be fragmented in small aspects, including:

Yoga Breathing

Yoga breathing includes long, deep breathing to remove the anxieties. Various techniques and methods play an important role in attaining mental peace and reviving energy. Breathing techniques in yoga are a key factor to attain an energy level that makes it work.

Yoga Mantra

Reciting yoga mantras over and over has its benefits. When you chant the mantra, it signals a chemical reaction to your body and mind. In this way, it will positively affect your mood. By chanting the mantra, you are energizing the power within yourself. It makes you confident, happy, joyful and opens up the chance to connect with divine energy. This mantra is accessible at any time in any form. You do not have to sit in meditation pose to chant mantras. You can chat while working or sleeping.

Yoga Kriya

Kriya means action; after you start with chanting and breathing, it is time to turn to action and perform the accompanying poses. It helps you achieve stamina in your body and boosts your confidence. You open your tensions and loosen up your body. You ultimately attain peace in your life. You make sure that you achieve the target that you want to get to through kriya.

Yoga is not a fast-acting activity, but it works slowly and steadily. It maintains your mental peace in a way that you wouldn't expect. You should have faith in your Kriya. It balances out your tension and makes you feel confident in your way.

Yoga Mudra

Yoga Mudra is an ancient practice of yoga particularly focused on different hand positions, locking and directing energy to different parts of your brain through them. The mudras generate energy through different postures of hands and fingers.

Once you master mudras, you feel confident and directed towards life. The confidence boost that you acquire is nothing but the faith you have in yourself that leaps from within as you achieve great success.

A very common type of mudra is Gyan Mudra. This type of mudra asks the practitioner to connect by pressing the index's fingernail into the thumb pad to stimulate energy and achieve calmness, brain expansion, and flow of energy in the body.

As you practice this mudra regularly, you enhance calmness and receptivity.

Yoga Meditation

Meditation has been associated with healing power for a long time. Whether you perform meditation for 3 minutes, 11 minutes, or 30 minutes, you will achieve specific results like altering electromagnetic fields around the body, stimulating blood circulation, and altering glandular and nervous systems simultaneously.

You can also perform meditation for 31 minutes to heal cells in your body, clear out the subconscious mind, and balance the rhythm of the body.

In ancient days, yogis were the masters of meditation, and they could stay in a meditative state for days, months, or even years. Well, it sounds unbelievable, but it is true. Meditation was the only source to make the soul meet with the divine energy, which is unseen by laymen. You cannot see but feel the entire process if you have awakened your Kundalini and balanced your Chakras.

Benefits of Awakening Chakras

Stress-Buster and Relieves Anxiety

Kundalini Yoga, including poses for chakra balancing, is a stress-buster that frees you from anxiety. A small study in 2017 showed great results where participants found relief from stress and anxiety while practicing chakra Yoga or Kundalini Yoga regularly.

Better Cognitive Functions

If you are suffering from mild cognitive impairment, you can improve with the regular practice of this kind of yoga. As you perform it daily, your memory and recall become strong, simultaneously enhancing other functions like problem-solving, reasoning, etc.

Boost in Self-Perception

These days, a myriad of people, especially youths, are prone to self-perception and body dysmorphia issues, which can result in them suffering from eating disorders. Practicing yoga makes you full of self-appreciation and improves self-perception. The practice of this yoga makes you feel self-love.

Spiritual Awakening

When you practice Kundalini yoga daily, you pave the way for spiritual awakening and enlightenment. With perseverance and practice, you become close to divine energy.

Here, being spiritual does not mean worshipping idols. It is to attain knowledge and wisdom through spiritual awakening. As you become fully awake, you will have gushing empathy, creativity, energy, and internal peace.

Balancing Chakras with Poses

Life is not a bed of roses. It may give you trouble at times which may sour the taste of life, making you feel miserable and mentally weak.

But, there is something which can help you out of this situation and help you regain the lost balance of life. You can achieve the target with the help of ancient yoga practices like chakra yoga.

With practice, you can attain mental peace and rejuvenate your energy. In the long run, the feeling of inner peace will resonate from the inside out, empowering you with mental and physical strength. Also, as you practice harnessing positive energy to the mind and body, you start to love yourself again and build a great self-perception of the world and people around you.

Shedding your old baggage will make you feel proud of yourself with no second thought about any choices you make from here on out. But, to achieve said benefits, all you need is to be determined and have strong willpower to continue the practices even if you feel yourself not wanting to.

Yoga's main goal isn't to make you lose weight, but it takes you to another energy level where clean living is something that everyone practices.

Practicing Clean Living

Clean living is a simple lifestyle that is free from worldly pleasures, needs, and desires. It is something that focuses on producing inner happiness—a life that is free from expectations and failures. There is no room for stress and anxiety. You will feel happy on the inside. You will get what you want to attain peace and love.

When you enter a yoga studio, you do not leave your problems at the door with your shoes. When you are on the yoga mat, you could feel bad, stressed, and overwhelmed. You need some kind of energy booster. With the right yoga class, one can feel light, refreshed, and clear. A good workout is the result of stress-busting. Many yoga teachers and ancient yogis feel that yoga poses and breathing exercises induce prana, i.e., life force, through your body.

According to the tradition of yoga, the subtle body is something that you cannot touch or see. In this body, there are seven points, and they are known as chakras. When energy is blocked in one chakra, there are imbalances in the emotional, mental, and physical systems of your physical body. It leads to poor digestion, anxiety, and lethargy. The asana practice frees the energy blocks and stimulates the body. With proper coaching, you can shift the energy and follow in the direction you want.

You must think of chakras as the access points to absolute self-care. Each chakra is associated with an element of nature. The founder of ISHTA Yoga, Alan Finger, explained that five chakras are related to earth, water, fire, air and ether or space. The last two chakras are associated with cosmic and light energy.

The well-being of your chakras makes life simple as you shed all materialistic and unnecessary elements from your life. You will find purpose in your life. It will give you strength and power. It will make life easy. You will find new meaning in life. Stress and depression will be far from you, and you will be more connected with your inner self. It will help you grow as a person. You will gain inner confidence that will lead to success in life. It is not a one-day activity. You need to practice it every day to attain chakra energy. You need guidance and support to do this properly.

Once you know the chakra and its related element, then you can start to feel that element in your body. It will help you restore fresh energy with entire practices. For example- root chakra is associated with earth. When this chakra is fortified with the necessary energy, you feel grounded and "rooted" to the earth. If it's out of balance, then you feel insecure.

The pelvic chakra is linked with water. When it is balanced, you feel your creative juices flowing unabatedly. If not, then you become rigid and emotionally brittle.

In order to begin the healing process, you need to first figure out which chakra needs stimulation to stop the imbalance. For example- if you are low in energy, then do yoga poses that target your navel chakra to stimulate the fire of your inner self. If you want the courage to speak the truth, then stimulate your throat chakra.

The practices that are chakra-based are tangible and create a ripple effect throughout yourself. The co-founder of Laughing Lotus Yoga Center, Jasmine Tarkeshi, is a Vinyasa Teacher and is practicing root chakra after becoming a mom. It has given her life-changing results and made her feel more grounded than ever.

You can perform the entire sequence, or you can focus on the poses that are specific to certain areas that need attention. First, close your eyes in a seating position and think of the color associated with chakra and radiate the chakra location. Then, you go deep with each asana and associate with the chakra sound while practicing yoga. The subtle changes cannot be measured physically, so it is up to you how honest you are with yourself and your progress. You must trust the inner experience to feel the change and even recognize the benefits.

London-based Yoga teacher Claire Missingham practices chakra-based yoga and keeps a journal. Keeping notes helps her to focus more and understand each point perfectly.

Chapter 7: Pranayama, Drishti, Asanas, Mantras and Mudras

Kundalini Yoga is an essential part of spiritual awakening. By mindfully observing the eight limbs of yoga, one can truly become aware of their inner self. Once this level of awareness has been achieved through the practice of yoga, it prompts the awakening of the Kundalini Shakti. In other words, the awakening of your dormant energy can be achieved through the regular practice of Kundalini yoga. In order to do so, you need to understand and utilize five techniques/concepts: Pranayama, Drishti, Asanas, Mantras, and Mudras.

Pranayama

It is the process of breathing and controlling one's breath during and after yoga poses. When translated from Sanskrit to English, "Prana" means energy or life, and "Yama" means expansion or control. Put together, pranayama means controlling life by allowing it to expand and flow. This is the fourth limb of yoga, and it works on three levels to help us achieve a fuller state of consciousness.

Benefits

Physically, pranayama regulates our breath. It helps slow down the heart rate and makes achieving an internal rhythm much easier. In the same way that you need to be mindful of your breathing in order to bring your heart rate down after an intense workout, being mindful of your breathing is the first step of being grounded in your physical realm.

Mentally and emotionally, pranayama helps calm down anxiety, stress, and restlessness. By regulating your breath and breathing through your diaphragm rather than your chest, you can deactivate your body's threat response. When stressed, the body favors using chest muscles for breathing as they are faster at providing oxygen. With enough awareness, you can notice when your body is stressed and ground yourself whenever you feel the need to. Simply being aware of how you breathe can help regulate your interactions with the life around you. Rather than out of anxiety and self-preservation, you can act out of love and compassion.

Spiritually, once you become conscious of the fact that, by breathing, you are letting life run its course inside and outside of your body, you access a deeper understanding of the union between mind, body, and soul. By noticing that breathing, in itself, is an act of love rather than a basic necessity, you can mindfully connect with yourself through each breath.

Pranayama for Kundalini Awakening

Kundalini Shakti is the energy dormant in your root chakra, Muladhara, which is located at the base of your spine. In order for it to be awakened, the life force (prana) needs to enter through your nadis (energy channels) and flow through your chakras. Prana is the most effective way to unblocking your nadis.

There are two techniques that are believed to purify the nadis, and these are samanu and nirmanu. Nirmanu is a physical cleansing that involves six purification rituals. Meanwhile, samanu is a meditation practice that combines controlled breathing with the use of mantras to prepare the body for pranayama. Once the nadis are pure enough, prana will flow through the chakras, and pranayama can be effectively practiced.

Kumbhaka Pranayama

This is a form of pranayama that depends on the subject's full retention of breath. As one inhales, they let in life. Once they choose to hold their breath, retaining life inside them without any distractions, they can achieve true stillness. According to the Yoga Institute, you should sit in the Sukhasana pose (cross-legged with an erect spine) and inhale smoothly for five seconds or as long as you feel your chest filled up. Retain your breath for double the amount of the inhalation time. Exhale gradually, slowly, and smoothly.

Ujjayi Pranayama

This second form of pranayama is intended to bring freedom from bondage, physical or otherwise. You start by sitting in the Sukhasana pose, then close your mouth and constrict your throat. Start inhaling, allowing air to pass through your constricted throat. Hold for double the inhalation time and exhale smoothly. Try to maintain a slow rhythm and keep your focus on the breath going in and out of your body. Remember, it's all about awareness, love, and compassion, so start slow with short inhalation and retention times, then work your way up. This process takes time, so be patient and kind with yourself.

Bhastrika Pranayama

The third form of pranayama is known for its ability to bring heat and warmth into the physical and the subtle body. After sitting in the Sukhasana pose, breathe in, then force the breath out of your nose (you should hear a hissing sound during the expulsion). Inhale again forcefully, then exhale with the same force. Make sure you use your abdomen and diaphragm. Don't substitute speed for quality. You still want to maintain deep and thorough breathing.

Kapalabhati

This is a cleansing technique intended to purify the sinuses. Simply stand with your hands hanging loosely by your side. Expel all the air in your lungs, then allow the air in through your nose. You will be exhaling forcefully, then allowing the air to go into your nose before you exhale it again. Note that you shouldn't retain your breath, as this is a cleansing process and not pranayama. As you might run out of breath, start with 15 rounds (inhale/exhale combination) of 30 seconds. In general, limit yourself to a maximum of three minutes; the process shouldn't take longer than that.

Drishti

Drishti stands for the focused gaze, but the aim is far from physical. By focusing your outward gaze on a fixed point in your mind during meditation, you limit your external stimuli and intentionally allow yourself to focus on your inner world. Your focused gaze is closely related to two of the eight limbs of yoga. The fifth limb, Pratyahara, is the withdrawal of the senses. It is centered on withdrawing the senses from the external world and pulling them inwards. The sixth limb,

Dharana, revolves around sustained concentration, and for that, maintaining a focused gaze is more than essential.

Maintaining focus can be done using a mantra, a candle or a symbol, or a statue as performed during trataka, focusing on a body part, or simply by breathing. When it comes to Kundalini awakening, inward concentration is important, as it fosters harmony between the mind, body, and soul. That said, there are eight gazes in Ashtanga yoga, each used with particular asanas (yoga poses). In Kundalini yoga, the eyes are closed, but one still uses their Drishti to direct the energy flow within their body.

Urdhva or Antara Drishti

This exercise is an example of a Drishti, where one's gaze is attached to a physical location rather than a point in or on the body. Urdhva, meaning upwards, is the focused gaze towards the sky. It is used in the asanas Warrior Pose I and II. It further promotes concentration, provides a feeling of expansion, and most importantly, it directs the flow of energy outwards.

Bhrumadhya Drishti

This is the third-eye focused gaze where the eyes are focused on a point slightly above the eyebrows and right in the middle, where your third eye lies. This Drishti activates the pituitary gland, improves concentration, and allows access to intuition.

Nasagra Drishti

This is a Drishti where the gaze is focused at the tip of the nose. It promotes concentration and stillness in the body. However, it shouldn't be practiced for more than three minutes at a time so as not to overstrain the eyes. Listen to your body. It's important for the eyes, as well as the facial muscles, to be relaxed while practicing Drishti. You'll find yourself naturally using this Drishti when doing an upward-facing dog pose (urdhva mukha svanasana).

Nabhi Chakra Drishti

When you direct your focus towards your navel and your nabhi chakra, which is when you successfully practice nabhi chakra Drishti. One commonly known pose that utilizes this Drishti is the downward-facing dog. By mastering the direction of your Drishti, you can better achieve balance and alignment within each pose, as well as direct your energy flow inward and through your chakras.

Angushthamadhyam Drishti

The Angushthamadhyam Drishti, which focuses on the middle of the thumb, is a very common drishti and one of the most prominently effective, thus helping beginners understand the concept of Drishti. By maintaining focus on the thumbs while doing an urdhva hastasana (upward salute), you allow for the full expansion of your spine. The point of focus also provides space for directing the attention inwards for the duration of the pose.

Hastagram Drishti

The hand and the fingertips are where this point of focus lies. This is yet another example of how drishti controls energy flow within the body. While doing an extended triangle pose, try directing your vision towards your hand as it is reaching towards the sky. Notice as the energy flows within you and observe your attention as it draws inwards.

Parsva Drishti

This is the second and third example of Drishti attached to a physical location. Parsva literally translates to "side". As we have two sides, left and right, Parsva Drishti is not comprised of one, but two, Drishtis. If you do an Ardha Matsyendrasana, your eyes should follow the direction you are turning your head in. However, it is important to maintain a balance between the right and left sides of the body through asanas and Drishtis. When doing an asana or focusing your gaze, don't forget to switch sides and adjust the pose and gaze accordingly so that a balance is established.

Padayoragram Drishti

This Drishti points attention towards the toes or the feet, grounding one's self and providing a calming stillness during spinal stretching that comes with many forward bends.

It is important to keep in mind that when trying to maintain concentration, that focus must come from within rather than force your mind to be still. Many beginners often make the mistake of trying to force themselves to concentrate, but the tension that comes with this process goes against the nature of yoga itself. When your mind loses concentration, which is very common, gently acknowledge your loss of focus and once more let go of your thoughts, then return your mind back to the present through focusing your gaze. However, you shouldn't force a gaze upon yourself either. Keep yourself relaxed and avoid straining your eyes. Remember the true purpose of drishti.

Asanas

Also known as a body posture in yoga, asana is the third limb of yoga. Before entering into deep meditation, one must physically prepare the body and ensure it is in a comfortable position. In order to reach Kundalini awakening, before you start practicing the fourth limb (pranayama), you must condition your physical body to be comfortable in each pose. According to the ancient text, Yoga Sūtras of Patañjali, asana should never feel strenuous or uncomfortable, as it defeats the purpose of the exercise. With enough practice, an uncomfortable asana can become comfortable. This comfort level is essential to practicing pranayama.

You may have seen or heard of asanas before, like the Padmasana (lotus pose), which almost everyone knows, and the Sukhasana mentioned above. Keep in mind, there is no single asana that works best, but rather a group of asanas that are designed to work in unison while preparing it for meditation sessions. Another key to properly practicing asanas is abandoning the competitive "yoga as a workout" mentality. Asanas spread balance. Performing them should be done slowly and mindfully with the intention of bringing about balance and promoting inward reflection. Yoga should not be practiced with the intention of weight loss.

While it is said, according to ancient texts, that there are 84 asanas, experts say that the exact number is unknown. There are, however, basic asanas, each designed to serve a specific purpose. In order to prepare your body for the Kundalini awakening, you need to practice asanas. Allow yourself the chance to struggle at first, then master the pose while properly regulating your breath. Here are several common types of asana:

Padmasana

This is a sitting asana in which the practitioner sits cross-legged with each ankle placed over the opposing thigh and their back erect. The soles of the feet need to be facing upwards and the ankles placed near the abdomen. Take great care not to overstretch your knee ligaments. When doing the full-lotus pose, use your hip joints instead of your knees. If you can't, try the easier half-lotus while you work on your flexibility through stretching your body.

Adho Mukha Svanasana

More commonly known as downward-facing dog, the adho mukha svanasana is an inversion pose. In order to properly execute the pose, place your head directly on the floor and stretch your arms outwards but keep them shoulder-width apart, same as your feet. Keep your legs as straight as you can, raising your hips well above your head. Your body should look like an inverted letter "V", and your weight should be distributed evenly on your hands and feet. In some variations, the head doesn't need to touch the ground. Remember to focus your Drishti towards your navel.

Shavasana

This is a reclining pose known as the corpse pose. It's a combination of relaxation and meditation; it isn't a physically demanding pose but one that promotes awareness through stillness. After lying on your back with your legs spread as wide as the mat, arms spread to the side, close your eyes, and let yourself breathe. Notice the tension within your body from your crown to your feet and let it go. Maintain the pose for any duration, from 5 to 30 minutes. When done with the asana, increase the depth of your breath, then flex your fingers and toes, reconnecting with your physical body. Reach your arms over your head, stretching your whole body. Exhale and press your knees to your chest, then lean to the side and get into a fetal position. Then, make your way to a seated position.

Shirshasana

The yoga headstand is classified as an inverted asana. Start with a 15-second child pose first to release any tension in your neck and shoulders. From there, place your elbows on the ground, in line with your shoulders, then interlock your fingers behind your head and cup your hands. Place the part of your head where your hairline meets your crown on the ground and let your cupped hands support the back of your head. Gradually, straighten your knees until your hips are in line with your upper body. Draw your knees, one by one, closer to your chest (your spine should be straight). Breathe in, then straighten your legs upwards and focus your gaze forward. Once you've gotten the hang of the pose, remind yourself to breathe. Start with thirty seconds of shirshasana, then work your way up to 3 to 4 minutes or more if you can. When coming down, do so slowly and with control, then end with a child pose.

Note: This asana is not recommended for people with lumbar/neck injuries, high blood pressure, or glaucoma. For pregnant women, the pose itself is not dangerous, but the risk of falling due to imbalance can harm you and the baby.

Mantras

Mantras serve many purposes, and they help activate Kundalini energy in more than one way. A mantra is not necessarily a phrase or affirmation, as it is commonly believed. In its simplest form, a mantra is a sound coupled with intention and devotion. It is a sound, word, or phrase uttered during yoga as part of a kriya (set of asanas, pranayama, mantras, and mudras). In itself, a mantra is a tool to fulfill several limbs of yoga.

The second limb of yoga, Niyama, is all about personal observances. Meaning it requires a great deal of introspection and devotion. One of the observances is Ishvara Pranidhana, surrendering the ego in exchange for the higher self. As we let go of our fixation on the ego, the I, or as psychologists define it, the part that tries to compromise between our needs wants, and social norms, we start connecting with the universe.

We gradually start abandoning shame, guilt, doubt, the desire-driven mentality, and instead, we become focused on our place in the universe. When we are freed from the bonds of desire and deep-rooted conditioning and open ourselves up to receive life within us instead. Chanting the mantra "Aum" with intention and devotion before and after a yoga session helps focus our concentration on the higher self as the sound "Aum" itself is the primordial sound, the sacred sound of the universe.

As any particle in the universe, we are constantly vibrating at a certain frequency. Mantras, being sounds at the end of the day, have their own unique frequencies. As you chant a mantra, you slowly start to vibrate in the same frequency as the mantra, on both a physical and a spiritual level. In a sense, by chanting "Aum", you are taking, or better yet, reclaiming your place as part of the universe.

Mantras are also incredibly useful when tending to Dharana, the sixth limb of yoga that revolves around concentration. When your mantra is a single sustained sound, it becomes easier to focus your mind by drawing attention to that stable stimulus, then gradually channeling that attention inwards. It functions in a way similar to Drishti, the focused gaze. In fact, in some meditations, mantra recitations are combined with candle gazing in order to further improve concentration.

Sat Nam

"I am one with Truth."

In Sanskrit, "Sat" means truth, and "Nam" means together. Literally, the phrase translates to "together with the truth", but it entails much more than that. Sat Nam is one of the most commonly used mantras in Kundalini yoga due to its power and ability to bring about transformation. By reciting to your mind that truth is your essence, you are solidifying a belief into your subconscious. Not just a belief that has the potential to make your life slightly better, but the main principle that drives the internal journey towards being truly awakened. It is only when we accept our truth that we can gain true awareness and access to our higher self. That's when the universal truth becomes attainable.

Ong Namo Guru Dev Namo

"I bow to the teacher within."

This is a mantra commonly recited three times at the beginning of each Kundalini yoga session. It prepares the yogi for the possibility of connecting with themselves. It grants them the ability to fulfill the Ishvara Pranidhana observance and surrender to their higher self, also known as the teacher within. The words hold within them great power, serenity, and confidence. It gives yogi the ability to observe their own shortcomings with compassion and their existence with love. "Ong Namo Guru Dev Namo" is considered to be a powerful mantra due to its high vibrations. When uttered in a group setting, it doesn't only unite the group with their own higher selves, but with each other as a collective. Overall, it deepens one's understanding and awareness of their truth and, in turn, helps them reach Kundalini awakening.

Mudras

While mudras are gestures or poses, they should not be confused with asanas. An asana is a physical pose meant to condition and benefit the physical body. Meanwhile, a mudra is sacred in nature and is specifically concerned with one's life force, their prana. It is designed to channel prana through the subtle body's nadis and chakras to awaken the dormant Shakti within. Keep in mind that mudra is still an external physical action, but the effects are internal, and this is why intention and devotion play a big role when practicing a mudra. Not just that, but it also takes a certain level of readiness to practice a mudra to its full effect.

Before one starts noticing the benefits of a mudra, they need to be physically prepared to commit to an asana, as well as the discipline and focus that comes with pranayama. Mudras channel prana within the subtle body's nadis, and so, if the nadis are not pure enough, a mudra wouldn't have much of a spiritual effect, rather a superficial, physical one.

That being said, even though there is a myriad of mudras, these are seven of the most common ones. Each comes with its own benefits and uses related to Kundalini awakening. You'll also find that most of them are based on the Hindu philosophy, which states that all creation is made of five basic elements: air, fire, water, earth, and space/ether. In the yogic tradition, each element is associated with a chakra. Because each of the five fingers is associated with an element, through hand mudras, one can regulate the energy of a particular element and its associated chakra(s).

Gyan Mudra

Perhaps the most common of all mudras, the gyan mudra stands for knowledge, focus, and wisdom. It is a simple hand gesture that seals in the prana within you as you are meditating. This energy seal is believed to promote balance within the heart chakra, sharpen focus, improve concentration, and increase awareness.

To practice this mudra, first sit in a padmasana or assume any other seated asana. Then, touch the tips of both your index fingers with your thumbs and stretch the three remaining fingers on each hand, but keep them relaxed. The backs of your hands should rest on your knees, and your palms should be facing upwards.

Prithvi Mudra

The prithvi mudra brings about balance and groundedness; spiritual, mental, and physical. It is connected to the earth element in the body, which, when in balance, displays itself in one's confidence, strength, and stability. By practicing the mudra, you can better balance and regulate the earth element and attain those goals.

As with the gyan mudra, if this is your first time performing the prithvi mudra, you need to assume a seated asana and lay the backs of your hands on your knees. All you need to do is touch the tips of your ring fingers to your thumbs while extending the rest of your fingers. Remember, don't forcefully straighten your fingers; simply extend them.

Shunya Mudra

The mudra is designed to regulate the element of space/ether within the body. Space is associated with three chakras: crown, third eye, and throat. It is mainly used for its health benefits to promote balance, alleviate inner ear problems and symptoms of vertigo/motion sickness.

To perform the mudra, assume a seated asana. Then, fold your middle finger, placing it at the base of the thumb, at the joint. Fold your thumb over your middle finger, using it to apply pressure on the middle part of the middle finger (between the first and second finger joints). The remaining fingers should remain outstretched yet relaxed.

Varuna Mudra

This is the mudra responsible for regulating the water element within the body. Due to the fact that 70% of the adult body is water, the varuna mudra has countless health benefits. These include relieving blood-related problems, kidney-related problems, and skin dryness. Most importantly, it activates and stimulates the sacral chakra.

After sitting in a padmasana or a sukhasana, rest your hands on your knees with the palms facing upwards. Then, touch the tips of your thumbs with the tips of the little finger. Stretch the other fingers without straining them.

Vayu Mudra

This mudra engages both elements, air (index) and fire (thumb). It helps settle the mind and restore peace, balance, and harmony within the body. Not to mention, there are some pressure points on the index finger that, when engaged, can have positive effects on the immune system and endocrine systems.

Sit in a padmasana or a sukhasana with your hands resting on your knees. Fold your index and place its tip at the base of your thumb. Then, fold your thumb over the middle part of the index finger. Keep the rest of your fingers gently stretched.

This brings us to the end of the kriya components necessary for awakening the Kundalini Shakti. As you practice asanas, pranayama, Drishtis, mantras, and mudras, make sure you do so with compassion, patience, and kindness towards yourself.

Chapter 8: Kundalini and Meditation

There are many kinds of yoga that fit and suit the needs and lifestyles of different individuals. Kundalini Yoga was introduced to the western world in the late 1960s by Yogi Bhajan, who introduced his own form of Kundalini Yoga to the United States in 1969. Kundalini practices started thousands of years ago when the first written teachings were dated back to around 500-800 BC, and it is widely believed that it was passed down as an oral tradition. However, scholars do not have a specific date on the exact origin of Kundalini practices. Before being introduced to the west, Kundalini practices were very private teachings, as they weren't known outside the circle of a select few teachers and their students, who were chosen after studying meditation and spirituality for many years. At first, Kundalini was composed of meditative teachings and techniques, and later on, yoga poses were included in the practices of Kundalini.

Kundalini is Sanskrit, which is an ancient Indo-European language that originated in the Indus Valley as early as 1500 BCE. It is also credited to being the predecessor for many Hindu languages that came after it. The word Kundalini in Sanskrit means "coiled" or "coiled snake". The rationale behind the name is the belief that each individual has dormant energy stored (coiled) at the bottom of the spine, and Kundalini meditation gives rise to this energy and releases it starting from the Sushumna Nadi (central core of the body) to the skull. Therefore, Kundalini energy release starts from the tailbone of the spine through the seven chakras until it reaches the crown chakra at the top of the skull. Kundalini meditation is believed to fully awaken a person's awareness. Thus, it has been dubbed as "Yoga of Awareness".

The Kundalini yogis believe that a person's will is the instrument of the soul, and through Kundalini Yoga, the physical, mental, and nervous energies in the body are harnessed under the domain of the will. Keep in mind that Kundalini yoga is not a religion but a way of life that, if applied to the human body and mind, can uplift its spirit. It brings balance to one's mind, body, and soul.

Kundalini Yoga Meditation

There are different kinds of Yoga and meditation techniques. However, what makes Kundalini Yoga meditation stand out from the rest is that it is precise, effective, and practical. Kundalini Yoga includes several extraordinary techniques like meditations to reduce stress, help with addiction, increase vitality, and clear the chakras.

Cleanse Your Mind

Kundalini meditation is viewed as a way to cleanse the mind the same way water cleanses the body. The best time for meditation is any peaceful time. However, the optimum time is before dawn in the early morning. When you start meditating, random and even unwanted thoughts will enter your awareness after a couple of minutes. Do not try to identify or focus on them; just let them pass. The more you meditate, the less these thoughts will affect your mind, thoughts, and emotions. The less these thoughts affect your life, the better quality of life you will have.

Stillness is the key to meditation. Being physically still will subsequently allow your mind to be in a state of peace, and when your thoughts become calm, you start to feel comfortable in your own skin. The more still and comfortable you are, the less these random, uninvited thoughts will be able to hit your awareness and cloud up your mind.

Since meditation is a process of cleansing your mind, you might face unpleasant thoughts or memories, which can make the cleansing process a difficult experience. However, to reawaken yourself and experience that "thing" that will bring awareness, calmness, along with an inner and outer change to oneself, you need to be patient. These ugly, unpleasant thoughts mean that the mantras and meditations are fulfilling their purpose, and you are being cleansed of the negativity that has been dampening the light within you. It is important to remain grounded while your mind goes through these kinds of thoughts to reach the awareness you are seeking.

As a general rule, you should be able to meditate anywhere. The state of your mind is of the highest importance and should not be constrained or hindered by your physical surroundings. The place you choose is not important as long as there are no distractions around you! You can meditate alone or with other yogis if you wish.

Meditation Guidelines

- There is no specific time for a successful meditative experience. Anytime that works for you is a good time to meditate, especially if it is at the same time every day. However, as mentioned above, it is recommended to meditate 2.5 hours before sunrise (the armit vela) because it is a reflective, quiet time by nature's standards. Performing early morning yoga sets you up for the rest of the day. Evenings and at sunset are considered a good time to meditate as well.

- The location where you meditate is very important. It needs to be a quiet place with no distractions and where you do not feel vulnerable. It is best to create your own spot for meditation and decorate it with objects that make you calm and uplift your spirit, be it candles, flowers, pictures, or whatever makes you feel cozy and inspired.

- Commitment is key to a successful meditation experience. However, it is ok if you miss a day, don't be too hard on yourself, just start again. Remember that even if you commit to only 3 minutes a day, it is better than a single 31 minutes session once a week. Regular practice and consistency are guaranteed to deliver results.

- When it comes to what you should wear while meditating, you can wear whatever makes you feel comfortable. Most people prefer loose, cotton clothing, and some even like to add a headcover. However, there are no rules here. Dress the way that feels right for you.

- Before starting your meditation journey, set your goals and intentions. The intensity of the power of meditation relies on your intentions. Why do you want to meditate? What is your desired effect? Focus on your goal so that the results can follow accordingly.

- Tune in with Adi Mantras before you begin. You can chant the phrase "Ong Namo Guru Namo" 3 times before you start meditating. While you are breathing, chant a mantra that would help you focus. It is recommended for beginners to chant "sat nam", which roughly translates to "I am the truth". Then, listen to yourself, or visualize the mantras being written on a piece of paper to direct your energy better.

- Focus on your breathing and gradually slow it down every session. The goal here is to make one cycle of breath (both exhaling and inhaling) last for about 7-8 seconds. Keep focusing on your mantras and breathing and if your thoughts wandered away, return your focus to your breath and mantra.

- When you finish your session, inhale deeply and push your arms together, finally relax and exhale.

Benefits of Kundalini Meditation

- It helps a person become more balanced and focused.

- Brings a person into a state of mindfulness.
- Balances mind, body, and soul.
- Improves the brain patterns and turns them into positive patterns.
- Builds up creative energy in oneself.
- Creates a state of awareness of the body.
- It helps in reducing anxiety.
- It helps a person find a sense of peace and releases stress.
- Enhances cognitive functions.
- Improves quality of sleep, especially with people who suffer from insomnia.
- Expands the lung capacity.
- Teaches the right way to breathe, which is into the diaphragm.

Featured Meditations

There are many featured Kundalini meditations like;

Kirtan Kriya

This kind of meditation is perceived as both a science and an art. Artistic, as it molds the consciousness and produces insights and a scientific due to the certainty of its results.

Kirtan Kriya results in a total mental balance. Moreover, if consistently practiced, it awakens the mind to the soul's infinite capacity. Some believe that if a person practiced Kirtan Kriya for 2-½ hours each day for a year while dressed in all white, they will know things unknowable to humans and see things that are invisible to the human eye.

Posture: Maintain a straight spine and sit in an easy pose. Put your wrists on your knees, arms, and elbows straight, start with the hands in Gyan Mudra. Your eyes should be at the brow point.

Mantra and Mudra: Chant Saa, Taa, Naa, Maa and alternate through 4 mudras. Each repetition should take 3-4 seconds. The first chant should be loud, followed by an audible whisper, then repeat the mantra in your mind. To complete the meditation, reverse the sequence, silently chanting, then whispering, then chanting loud.

Time: 11-31 minutes. If you are practicing for 31 minutes, each verbalized chant should take 5 minutes, and the internal chant should be approximately 19 minutes. For shorter durations, maintain the same proportions.

Meditation for Beaming and Creating the Future

The best way to do this is on an empty stomach, with the only exception being fluids, like water or tea. This kind of meditation states that when the mind is clear from all the distractions and attachments, it beams and stays focused, and it shows its incredible capacity and potential of creativity. A person practicing this kind of featured Kundalini meditation becomes still and then dedicates their mind to focus on their future and relationships with the outer world.

Posture: Keep your spine straight, stay very still, and sit in an easy pose while your eyes are closed. Relax your hands in Gyan Mudra on your knees.

Part 1: Take a single, deep breath through a rounded mouth. Close your mouth and exhale through your nose slowly but completely. Keep doing that for 7-15 minutes.

Part 2: Inhale and hold your breath. When you suspend your breath in, meditate on zero. Meditate on the negative emotional and physical conditions and bring them to zero. Then, exhale and repeat. Breath in a comfortable rhythm.

Part 3: Think of a condition that you desire the most. Try to formalize that desire in one word, "health", for example. Lock that word in and visualize it. Then, inhale and suspend your breath as you resonate this thought in a continuous manner. To end the meditation, inhale and move your shoulders, arms, and spine. Stretch your arms and spread your fingers wide. Finally, breathe a couple of times deeply.

Meditation for a Calm Heart

Meditation for a Calm Heart includes soothing pranayama (breathing practice) that relieves anxiety and creates mental clarity and a state of calmness. On the emotional level, "Meditation for a Calm Heart" gives a clear perception of relationships. On the other hand, physically, it strengthens the heart and lungs.

Posture: Pick a relaxed pose, like the lotus pose, while maintaining a light Jalandhar bandh and place your left hand on your chest at the center of the heart. Keep the palm flat against your chest. Your right hand should be held up slightly above shoulder level, with your palm facing outwards and your index finger pressed into your thumb pad. Relax your elbows and keep your forearms perpendicular to the ground.

Close your eyes or look straight ahead while with your eyes 1/10 open of the way.

Breath: Inhale slowly but deeply through your nostrils. Hold your breath and raise your chest. Stay that way as long as possible. Then exhale gradually and fully. When the air is completely out of your lungs, refrain from inhaling again as long as safely possible. Focus on your breath flow and regulate each breath consciously.

To end the meditation session, inhale and exhale 3 times strongly, then relax.

Healing the Wounds of Love

This kind of meditation creates sounds as mantras by using verses. These mantras were originally written in the form of letters between Guru Arjan and Guru Ram Das. When someone repeats these mantras, it takes them away from the normal internal chatter and the emotional mind games in order to align, strengthen, and purify the heart and soul. Doing this meditation 11 times each day for 11 days will drop the pain and fill you with clarity and authenticity.

Mantra: The first 4 stanzas of Shabad Hazaray.

Facing the Challenge of Tomorrow:

To face tomorrow's challenges, we need to live in the present moment and accept what it brings.

Posture: Keep your spine straight and sit in an easy pose.

Part 1: Keep your arms straight out to the sides. The elbows should stay at the same level as your shoulders while your palms are facing down. Bend your elbows in. There should be a stretch felt in the armpits. Then, close your eyes and focus them on the tip of your chin. Breathe deeply and slowly. Repeat that process for 3 minutes.

Part 2: Stay in the same position and turn your palms up to the ceiling. Continue for 3 minutes.

Part 3: Turn your palms to face the sides. The thumb should be facing down. Keep your arms at shoulder level. Continue for 3 more minutes.

Part 4: Finally, inhale and hold your breath while squeezing your muscles. Exhale and repeat the same sequence two more times, then relax.

Meditation for Spiritual Stamina

During this meditation, the spine must be straight and the hands held over the head throughout the process in order to cover the magnetic field of the body. During the first couple of minutes, you might feel discomfort. However, when the pain passes, you will enter an incredible state of relaxation.

Posture: Sit in a comfortable crossed leg sitting position.

Mudra: The fingers should be interlaced and arms raised over your head with your palms facing down. Bend your elbows until they reach 6 inches from the crown of the head. Your eyes should be 1/10th open.

Breath: Inhale deeply, then hold your breath for as long as you safely can. Exhale and refrain from inhaling for as long as possible. Continue doing this for 11 minutes, and once comfortable, gradually increase the time to 31 minutes.

Blessing Meditation

To be able to bless ourselves, we need to be able to bless others around us. In order to do this, we need to see the divine in all. This form of meditation is often used by priests to bless others. Throughout the meditative state, they will chant the mantra "May the Jupitar energy as Guru, and the Saturn energy as Guru, be with you".

Part 1: Start by sitting in a lotus pose, spine straight, chin in, and chest out. Then, bend your elbows to your sides, and bring your hand up until they are six inches away from each ear. Palms should be facing forward and fingers pointing to the ceiling. Make your hands into fists and extend the index and middle fingers straight up, all the while keeping your hands by your side. Keep your eyes closed. Then, play the Prosperity Hymn and sing along.

Part 2: Stretch your arms over your head, and keep your elbows straight. Make hands into fists while extending the index and middle fingers straight and bring the tips of both together. Then, play Humee Hum Brahm Hum and sing along. Stay this way for 6.5 minutes, then inhale and hold your breath for 10 seconds. Exhale, then inhale again but immediately move to part 3.

Part 3: Fold your hands in the Prayer Pose. Keep your palms flat at the center of the heart. Then, play Ong Namo Guru Dev Namo and sing along. Stay still for 1.5 minutes and finish it up by inhaling and relaxing.

Meditation to Learn to Pray

This meditation is very special as it allows you to focus on the need to have your whole mind present and influencing your own vibration.

Mudra: First, interlace your fingers and keep your left pinkie on the outside. Extend both your index fingers up. Then, cross your thumbs, putting the right one over the left. Put your thumbs close to your chest with the index fingers pointing up to the ceiling. Your elbows should be bent. Eyes should be closed or 1/10th open.

Focus: Imagine yourself being at peace, and breathe slowly and deeply. Imagine that this still, radiant image of yourself is sitting on the peak of Mount Everest, and you're a glowing pillar of energy. Picture a bright light connecting the base of your neck and the base of your spine. Finally, picture that light pouring itself into the universe around you.

Time: 11 to 31 minutes maximum.

To finish the session, increase the amount of air you exhale and inhale for one minute while holding your position to wake your body. Then, stretch your arms to the sides. Your arms should be at shoulder level, while your palms face down and your elbows are both bent at a 45-degree angle. Start circling your hands, right hand counterclockwise and left hand clockwise. Flutter your fingers like you are sending the energy to the environment surrounding you.

Meditation to Remove Fear of the Future

It is common for humans to feel fear of the unknown, and the subconscious holds onto that fear and internalizes it, which can limit our potential and have a negative impact on the quality of our lives. This meditation takes away those fears and allows you to focus and deal with your heart center.

Posture: Find a comfy place and sit in a lotus pose.

Mudra: Put the back of your left hand on the palm of the right hand. The right thumb should be nestled within the palm of the left hand while the left thumb crosses over it. Curve the right-hand fingers around the outside of the left hand. Rest the side of your palm against your chest and put this mudra at the center of your heart.

Mantra: Find your favorite version of Dhan, Dhan, Ram Das Guru and meditate to it.

Time: 11 minutes is perfect for a start and then gradually move up to 31 minutes.

To end this meditation, inhale deeply and relax.

There are many more kinds of featured Kundalini Meditation that you can choose from, like Meditation for Maturity and Wisdom, Meditation for Spiritual Stamina, Open Lotus Heart Meditation, each serving their own unique purpose to better your quality of life. Remember that if you are going to practice in your home and on your own, you need to tune in with the Adi Mantra and follow the Kundalini Yoga Meditation guidelines.

Yogic Science

As per yogic science, meditations and exercises done in a kriya should be done during a specific time frame because each desired effect of meditation has a specific period when it is at its most effective. Below is the time length needed for different meditation purposes:

- **3 minutes:** These 3 minutes have an effect on the blood circulation, stability of the blood chemistry, and electromagnetic field.

- **11 minutes:** Changes the nerves and glandular system.

- **22 minutes:** This results in balancing and coordinating the three minds (negative, positive, and neutral), which changes the mental integration.

- **31 minutes:** Affect the mind's projection layers, body cells, and body rhythms. Moreover, meditating for 31 minutes balances the 3 gunas and 31 tattvas.

- **62 minutes:** Results in integrating the subconscious and the outer projection. Also, 62 minutes can change the gray matter of the brain.

- **2.5 hours:** Surrounds the universal mind, thus, holds the new pattern in the subconscious. These 2.5 hours can change the psyche in relation to the magnetic field surrounding it.

Making meditation a daily routine will teach you to master obtaining its effects. Moreover, repetition tends to turn things into a habit. The cycles of the human mind could be used to help replace the unwanted patterns of behavior with a positive pattern. There are many meditations to choose from. Set your goal, choose a meditation that serves that goal, then commit to practicing it over 40 days to change a habit, 90 days to confirm that habit, 120 days to gain this as a new habit, or 1000 days to master the new habit!

Chapter 9: Different Kundalini Exercises

As you've learned throughout the previous chapters of this book, you need to focus on a number of different elements when practicing Kundalini yoga. Beginners who jump straight into the physical aspect of Kundalini yoga without paying attention to the rest of the elements miss out on the essence of this spiritual practice. In this chapter, you will get to learn about some of the most common Kundalini exercises and how you can benefit from each and utilize them in your journey to achieve Kundalini awakening.

How to Prepare Before Kundalini Exercises

Before getting into the different elements of Kundalini yoga and the different exercises that you can perform, you need to adjust your surrounding environment to guarantee the best possible results. Here are tips to keep in mind before you start:

- **Find the best location:** Unless you're an advanced yogi who can separate themselves from anything around them and solely focus on their breath and movement, you have to find a quiet location. If you'll be practicing from your home, choose your favorite corner or room and set up there. Your chosen space should be neat and comforting enough to support the spiritual aspect of your practice. Adjust your room temperature, never too cold or too hot, so you don't get distracted.

- **Find the best time:** There's no right or wrong time for doing Kundalini exercises. We're all different, so what works for your friend won't necessarily work for you and vice versa. You should find the time of day where you are most in tune with yourself and are usually in a receptive state of mind to reap the benefits of Kundalini. Ideally, you'd practice first thing in the morning or last thing before bed. Try to avoid the midday hustle when it's noisy outside and you've just had your lunch. If you can, try to fix the timing of your practice every day to encourage consistency and build up momentum as you move forward.

- **Wear the right clothes:** Again, there are no hard-set rules when it comes to choosing your exercising attire. However, it would be nice to pay attention to the small details and follow in the footsteps of Kundalini masters, wearing all-white flowy clothes, for example. The color white is synonymous with peace and tranquility, which are exactly the feelings you would want to evoke when performing Kundalini exercises. Some advanced practitioners like to wrap a white turban around their heads in an attempt to trap in the emitting energy and stop it from escaping through the head. As a beginner, you might find the turban limiting to your movement, so keep it for future use when you become more advanced. To summarize, you should wear something breathable and light in color that gives you a full range of motion and makes you feel comfortable in your skin.

- **Use supportive props:** Later in this chapter, as we move on to the actual exercises, you'll notice that you'll be holding each pose for a few minutes at a time. So, in order to make sure you stay comfortable and undistracted, you should consider using supportive props like a pillow or a blanket for extra cushioning. Because Kundalini is all about maintaining a meditative state, try not to create a fuss around you with too many props. If you find them distracting and disrupting your process in any way, it's better to get rid of them altogether.

- **Decide on the length of your practice:** You don't have to perform Kundalini exercises for hours on end for the energy to start flowing in your body. Sometimes a 3-minute exercise is all you need to make that happen, especially if you're a regular practitioner. Whichever level you are at, before you start, you should decide on the intended length of your practice to set your mind's expectations and encourage it to cooperate for better results.

- **Pick a mantra:** With all the inhaling and exhaling you'll be doing throughout your exercises, it's recommended to pick a mantra that speaks to you in a way. It's a great way to make you focus on where you want to be rather than where you currently are. For example, one of the most common mantras used during Kundalini exercises is "Sat Nam", which roughly translates to "I am the truth", or "The truth is me." Every time you inhale, repeat out loud or in your head the word "Sat", and as you exhale, the word "Nam". You'll be surprised at how soothing using a mantra is during practice and how it can take you even further.

- **Be Mindful of your breathing:** Normally, breathing is considered to be a passive activity; you don't exactly think about inhaling and exhaling while you're driving or watching TV. However, breathing in Kundalini and all other types of yoga is rather different. It's more of an active action that you have to be mindful of. Let every breath you take be intentional with the sole purpose of fueling your body to be able to move and flow. As for your exhales, they should also be intentional to empty out your lungs and relax you back into your starting position.

The Elements of Kundalini Yoga

To better prepare yourself for the different poses and exercises, it's imperative that you learn about each of the preparatory Kundalini yoga elements. Here they are:

1. **Starting with a chant:** Any true Kundalini practice should start with an opening chant to help you get in tune with yourself and shift your focus

inwards in preparation for your practice. If you're unfamiliar with chanting and you're unsure where to start, you can refer back to chapter seven and revisit the part about mantras and how chanting them can heighten your senses and make you feel more connected. A simple Om chant is a good place to start until you get used to the idea of chanting. A correct Om chant should feel like pulsating energy traveling from your pelvic floor all the way up to your head, inviting feelings of peace and calmness throughout into your entire body. Don't be discouraged or feel self-conscious if your Om's don't sound confident or soothing enough at first. With continuous practice, you'll be able to get over this hesitation as chanting becomes more of a second nature to you.

2. Warming Up: Just like any exercise, you can't start without warming up, more so with Kundalini as you're warming up on 3 levels. A physical, mental, and spiritual warm-up is essential before you can move onto your different poses and asanas. Think of it this way, if you want to invite the mighty Kundalini energy to flow smoothly throughout your body, you have to make way and clear any "obstructions", and this is exactly what a good warm-up should do. However, warming up for Kundalini yoga is slightly different because it's all about regulating your breath or your pranayama, as explained in previous chapters. You should also incorporate stretching to open up your muscles and release any tension in your body. If you plan on practicing on your own at home, here's a typical Kundalini warm-up sequence to get you started:

- After finishing your chants, sit in either an easy pose or half-lotus where you cross your legs and sit comfortably with your hands on your knees and your spine straight like a bind. If you're doing it correctly, you should feel as if you got a few inches taller, feeling a nice stretch from your lower back all the way to the nape of your neck. Once you feel centered and stable enough, start rolling your pelvis as much as you can in both directions while maintaining a steady flow of breath. You can inhale as you rotate and exhale as you go back to the center. Try to breathe deeply to get into a meditative state and start traveling inwards. Do this move for a couple of minutes, no more than 3. Then relax for 30 seconds to reset your energy before you move forward. This move maintains the health of your internal organs and gently starts to release the energy surrounding your lower spine.

- While you're in the same seated position, start doing spinal flexes. It's like doing a typical cat-cow sequence, but instead of being on all-fours, you're sitting with your legs crossed. With your hands on your ankles, as you inhale, let the air open up your chest and feel as if your shoulders are expanding and getting wider. Then exhale, release the air rounding your shoulders forward. Make sure your head doesn't bob up and down as you move; try your best to keep it resting comfortably over your shoulders to allow your breath to flow easily. Repeat this move for a few minutes, or you have the choice to keep going until you can feel the energy starting to move freely throughout your body, especially around your spinal area. For your last round, take a deep inhale, hold it for a few counts before you finally release, and get back to a neutral position.

- You can either stand up or continue in your easy pose to do side twists. Put your hands over your shoulders, keeping your elbows straight and parallel to the ground, then start rotating your core the same way you did in the first warm-up move. Make your side-twists deep with your head moving along with your core in a grinding motion. Don't stiffen your hands over your shoulders; instead, let them rest with your arms moving as a result of your core twisting and not on their own accord. You can make this move for a couple of minutes before you finally inhale deeply, facing forward, then exhale, relax and take note of how energy has traveled upwards towards your heart, opening it up.

- Again, either remain seated in your crossed-leg position or sit back on your heels for neck rolls and shoulder shrugs. Relax your shoulders, and hold your neck tall without adding any tension to it, then let the weight of your head take the lead, gently leaning it back as you inhale from right to left, then exhale, dropping your head forward, chin to chest rotating from left to right. Repeat for one minute, then reverse and move in the other direction for another minute. When you're done, relax and sit back, you should be feeling a nice release in your neck.

- To relax and release tension from your shoulder while seated, inhale, lifting your shoulders upwards, then exhale as you drop them down. Continue this movement for a couple of minutes, then take a deep breath before you let it out and relax, shifting your focus onto your shoulders feeling the sweet sensation of tension release around that area.

- Moving on to the legs. For the life nerve stretch, sit with both legs stretched forward. Start by tucking the right foot into the left thigh as you take a deep breath in. Straighten your spine, then exhale, start folding forward, grabbing your feet with your hands if you can. If this is too challenging for you, lean forward with your back straight. Once you feel like you're hunching over, readjust until you find a comfortable position. Finish one whole minute on each side, then start shaking your legs while seated, giving them a quick massage to promote blood circulation. The life nerve stretch has several benefits, including strengthening your core, strengthening reproductive and digestive organs, and loosening up your leg muscles. As beneficial as this move is, it's better not to attempt it if you gave birth less than 120 days ago, are suffering from pregnancy complications, or on the first few days of your cycle.

- Finally, you can wrap up your warm-up with the infamous cat-cow pose. Come onto all fours with your hands firmly on the ground hip-width apart. Take a deep breath in, arch your back, lift your head up and look upwards, then exhale out, round your back all the way up, pulling your head down and shifting your gaze towards your feet. To make sure you're doing this right, try to be a bit dramatic and articulate your movements. Do cat-cow for 1-3 minutes. To finish, take one final cow stretch while inhaling, then exhale, sit back onto your heels, relax and try focusing on your mind's eye.

3. Performing Kriyas: In Kundalini yoga, kriyas refer to a series of poses, asanas, and mudras (as explained in earlier chapters) paired with various breathing techniques or pranayama as you know them by now. In other words, this is the meat of your practice. It's where you get to bring the main components of your practice together. Think of it as the time where the magic happens after having warmed up and prepares your body to open up, inviting Kundalini energy to flow freely through you and before winding down and closing your practice. According to your instructor or your own preference if you are practicing on your own, the intensity and duration of your kriyas can be adjusted accordingly. The important thing is to make it strenuous and long enough to help you get with yourself and feel the Kundalini awakening bit by bit.

4. Relaxing: Relaxation is a big part of any Kundalini practice, especially after performing a series of challenging kriyas; you have to take a few minutes to relax and recenter yourself before moving into a meditative state as you move towards the end of your practice.

5. Meditating: For beginners, meditating can be a little intimidating. Don't be surprised if you find the strong part of Kundalini yoga-where you move and flow-much easier than sitting still alone with your thoughts. It actually takes a lot of practice, sometimes even years, before you can get to the point where you can observe your passing by without the need to engage with them. Meditating is not about clearing your mind until it's blank and free of thought because that's actually impossible. It's more about getting into a submissive state, accepting your thoughts for what they are, and letting them be without engaging with them. If you're a beginner, consider practicing with an instructor to guide you through mindful meditation sessions.

6. Closing chant: Much like how you first started, your Kundalini practice should be concluded with a closing chant. If you were hesitant with your opening chant, you'd find yourself more confident with your closing one. That's because by closing time you would've already summoned enough Kundalini energy to boost your mood and open you up.

Different Kundalini Exercises

Now you're ready to get into the actual exercises of Kundalini yoga. The section below should guide you through a wholesome practice that you can rely on as a beginner. However, don't feel like you should be able to perform each of the poses to the fullest and with the same level of efficiency. If your hips are tight, for example, folding forward with your legs wide-apart can be quite challenging. So, remember to make adjustments with each exercise to make it suitable for your current level. You can then build up as you advance and your body gets used to this kind of movement. Let's get started:

Lotus Pose

This is one of the basic poses in yoga. Although it looks simple, it can be quite strenuous on the inner thighs and hips if you're usually tight in these areas. To get into the lotus, sit comfortably with your legs extended first. Then, bend your right knee bringing your right foot to rest on your left thigh. Do the same with your left knee, this time, resting your left foot on your right thigh. Once you feel grounded and stable, straighten your spine, close your eyes, and start breathing in and out deeply. Try to connect with your breath and feel that each inhale is opening you up, and the exhale is bringing you back to your center. If you prefer, you can bring both of your hands to your heart center in a prayer mudra. You can start chanting your mantra out loud or in a whisper, whichever makes you feel more present.

Cobra Pose

Lying down on your stomach, with your arms close by your side and your palms resting against the floor. Then slowly rise up, straightening your arms, lifting your torso, and kneecaps off the ground balancing on your toes. Make sure your elbows are tucked in, your fingers are facing forward, and your neck is long and lifted facing upward-if you can. Finally, hold for 30 seconds at a time before you release and rest. Cobra is not always the most comfortable of poses because it requires upper-body strength and good balance. However, it's believed to be very beneficial in activating Kundalini energy in the body. If you can't manage to hold for 30 seconds at the first attempt, start with 10 and build up as you progress, just like we recommended at the beginning of this section.

Stretch or Low-Boat Pose

With your back straight on the floor, tighten your legs to point your toes and hold them straight together. Using your core strength, lift your legs a few inches off the ground. Then do the same with your head and upper body. Keep your hands parallel to your upper body, with the palms facing one another. Hold this pose for a few minutes or for however long you can. Whatever you do, do not hold your breath in because you'll have the tendency to do so as you try to keep yourself from losing your balance. If you want to take this pose further, try doing the "breath of fire" instead of regular breathing. "Breath of fire" is a forceful exhalation breathing technique. You take a small breath in and then rhythmically start exhaling the air out in short pants, feeling your core tighten each time. Even though this is an excellent pose, you should skip it if you're pregnant, as the pressure can put your baby's life at risk.

Archer Pose

From the name, you can understand what this pose is all about. In this pose, you assume a position similar to that of a warrior. Start by standing straight facing forward, then slowly move your right foot outward and take it to the back at a 45-degree angle until it lands straight behind you. Bend your left knee, making sure it doesn't go past your toes. As for your arms, straighten them both and lift them to shoulder height. Close your fists, pointing your thumbs up as you rotate your torso toward the left with the right elbow bending as if you're holding an imaginary arrow. Look forward, plant your feet to the ground and start pacing your breath, holding this pose for a few minutes. Repeat the same after switching sides, then hold again for a few minutes. As you open up your chest holding the strong archer pose, you will feel confident and ready to receive all the Kundalini energy that will pass through your body. Furthermore, this pose is said to activate your 3rd chakra, which is all about strong willpower and self-esteem. Do this pose whenever you're going through times of uncertainty and hesitation, and you'll see for yourself how much it's going to help you.

Hold Your Toes

Sitting on the floor with your legs extended forward, start opening your legs wide to the opposite sides. Once you can't open any further, flex your toes toward your body, raising your arms up and straight to frame your head. Hold this pose, breathing in and out for a few minutes before you start folding forward. Keep your back straight as you start leaning forward with your chest toward the floor and each of your hands extended to hold your toes. With every inhale, lift up your head and torso; as you exhale, try to make your forehead touch the floor. Repeat the movement for a few minutes before you relax back to the center position. This pose stretches your legs, especially the hamstrings and calves. It also improves digestion and massages your lower back.

Venus Mudra

In this pose, you sit back on your heels, holding your back upright and straight. Interlace your fingers in front of you in Venus mudra with your palms resting on your lap. As you inhale, stretch your hands all the way above your head, exhale, move it down mindfully, resting your hands back on your lap. Continue this movement for 1-3 minutes before you rest back in the center. Venus mudra is associated with sensuality; this pose can help restore your glandular balance and also promotes better concentration.

Ego Eradicator

Ego eradicator is one of the most popular Kundalini exercises. Seated in an easy pose, straighten your arms with your fingers folded inward and both thumbs pointing up. Raise your arms at a 60-degree angle above your head. Breathe in and out with your eyes closed. If you can, it's better to do the "Breath of fire" prana with this pose. Hold for 1-3 minutes, take in a deep breath touching both thumbs above your head, then finally release. Ego eradicator does wonder in balancing your sympathetic and parasympathetic nervous systems. It also helps clear your lungs and strengthen your navel chakra.

If you're still building up your Kundalini practice, the above exercises are a great place to start as a beginner. They're simple enough yet very effective in activating Kundalini energy to flow throughout your body. In the next chapter, you'll get to learn all about the marvelous benefits of Kundalini awakening and why you should consider making this type of yoga part of your physical and spiritual exercise routine.

Chapter 10: Kundalini Awakening and Its Effects

Mystics, yogis, and spiritual leaders believe that every human being who is born has a purpose to fulfill. It is believed that the true potential of a human being needs to be discovered and activated consciously. Many practices can help an individual find their life's purpose and activate their full potential. Many of these practices are ancient and truly powerful. Whenever someone taps into the energy within them, it can magically transform their life. This personal and spiritual unfolding process is also known as awakening or enlightenment.

All forms of life adapt, change, transform, and evolve constantly. Everything in our universe is in a continuous state of transformation. To yearn for personal and spiritual transformation means leaving behind the monotony and stagnancy of their current state. An awakened or an enlightened being always beams with vitality and is full of life. Enlightenment or awakening is not only a transcendental state of living but also a continuous process. Just like how plants and trees shed their leaves to give birth to new ones, we humans must also shed the beliefs and stigmas that limit our access to the life force. When a person is free of all their self-imposed limitations, they're awakened to better and higher dimensions of life. When an individual is enlightened by the true nature of all life forces, the feelings of peace, prosperity, and contentment can easily be found and held on to.

No matter if a person chooses to realize their true potential or continues living in incomprehension, our souls will always long for growth and transformation. This longing, if ignored for too long, can depress the energy present within the body, making it more difficult to access it. Without conscious effort, the energy will continue to be dormant. Awakening is all about listening to our inner voices and consistently exploring the world around and within us. The more aware a person is, the more joy and vitality they experience in their life.

Awakening is similar to how we wake up in the morning. By simply opening our eyes, we can take in our surroundings. The only difference between waking up and awakening is that you'll need to open your inner eyes instead of the physical eyes to be awakened to the various dimensions of life. Our lives continue to expand when we allow ourselves to start seeing the world with our inner eyes. The infinite possibilities of life open up, and every moment is an opportunity to feel divine energy coursing through your veins.

What is Kundalini Awakening?

Several different pathways can lead us to divine enlightenment. In Buddhism, the spiritual practice of attaining peace and wisdom is known as *nirvana or bodhi*. Interestingly, the literal translation of the name *Buddha* is "the one who knows, understands, and is awake". Here, awakens refers to the spiritual awakening of a being. Similarly, in the Vedic literature of Hinduism, the practice of spirituality is known as *tapas or sadhana*. Both the ancient teachings of Buddhism and Hinduism allow you to navigate the spiritual pathways towards your enlightenment.

Kundalini yoga is one such ancient practice that helps human beings discover their life's purpose, live to their fullest potential, and channel the limitless energy that resides in a coiled state at the base of their spine. The word Kundalini is derived from the Sanskrit word "Kundal", which means "coiled up like a snake", The sleeping or dormant energy form in our bodies can be awakened through a systematic combination of yoga asanas (poses), kriyas (exercises), mantras (chanting), and breathing techniques. By practicing Kundalini yoga, the seven prime energy junctions of our bodies, also known as the seven chakras, can be tapped into. The process of activating the seven energy centers in our body can lead a human to experience and explore life to the fullest. This process of expanding our consciousness and making use of the limitless divine energy at our disposal is known as Kundalini Awakening.

A Brief History of Kundalini Awakening

In ancient cultures of the Indus Valley, as depicted in the Upanishads (sacred Vedic collection of teachings, dated around 1000 B.C. to 500 B.C.), Kundalini was a study of spirituality, philosophy, and the science of energy before it developed into a physical practice. According to the ancient collection of writings, Kundalini masters would sit with royals and other students to spread their knowledge of enlightenment. It was considered an advanced method of attaining nirvana or moksha and was not privy to the public. Disciples of great Kundalini masters would gather to listen to the oral recitations of the spiritual experiences witnessed by the masters. It is noted that students had to prepare for years before they were initiated in the practice of Kundalini awakening.

The science and practice of Kundalini were veiled in utmost secrecy until very recently. The divine knowledge was well hidden by elite yoga practitioners since they believed that such powerful knowledge could be dangerous in the grasps of the untrained minds of unguided students. However, the sacred knowledge that was once not allowed to be shared outside the Indian yogic lineage was brought to light by the revered Yogi Bhajan and especially gained traction when the hippie movement was picking up speed in the west.

In the late 1960s, when Yogi Bhajan was visiting the United States, he had a vision during one of his meditation sessions. The vision showed him a path to combine the ancient knowledge of Kundalini with the practicality of modern healing. Inspired by the vision he had, Yogi Bhajan went on to establish 3HO (Happy, Healthy, Holy Organization), as well as the Kundalini Research Institute, where he conducted over 10,000 Kundalini yoga sessions. Yogi Bhajan personally trained thousands of people, some of whom went on to become well-known Kundalini teachers themselves. It is vital to acknowledge that without Yogi Bhajan, the sacred knowledge of Kundalini awakening would have remained a mystery to the Western world. The U.S. Congress honored him posthumously for his priceless contributions to the modern world.

The Philosophy of Kundalini Awakening

Also known as the Yoga of Awareness, the philosophical purpose of Kundalini awakening is to open oneself to the spiritual nature of reality. The concept of Kundalini can be traced back to the ancient literature of the Upanishads. Kundalini awakening in its real essence means being awakened to one's higher self. The numerous scientific practices developed by the masters of Kundalini yoga over the centuries help us push past our self-destructive traits and unite with the eternal universal energy.

In traditional Kundalini yoga teachings, instead of being a personified deity, the essence of god is understood as the consciousness or the energy that endlessly flows through the universe. The divine nature of this powerful energy can be accessed by anyone since humans are partly made up of said. By separation and detachment from the human ego, one can experience the real connection that all humans have with the universe and understand the true nature of their existence.

How is Kundalini Awakened?

Several ways can lead to Kundalini awakening. For some, it may take years of dedicated practice, while some may experience Kundalini awakening spontaneously. In Hinduism, there are a variety of holy practices that can help achieve Kundalini awakening. Several people in India leave their homes and lives behind to become yogis. They spend years cleansing themselves and preparing for the experience of Kundalini awakening. Rigorous preparations and regular nutrition are required for safely and properly awakening the

Kundalini. It is believed that the awakening of Kundalini cannot be controlled. You can't know if, or when, you're Kundalini will awaken. All you can do is prepare for it and be receptive to the change when the Kundalini awakens.

While Kundalini awakening is a very positive process, it can also bring a lot of intense experiences. The essence of Kundalini awakening lies at the core of our body. A life force energy is believed to be lying dormant at the base of our spines. By consciously tapping into that energy, you can make it rise from the base of your spine towards the crown. As the prana rises through your spine, you can feel the energy within yourself rising, too. The awakened energy courses through our body like electricity, charging up the nervous system of your body. When the energy within your system is at its peak, the process of Kundalini awakening takes place.

To understand the process of Kundalini awakening in a simpler way, consider the dormant life force energy to be a coiled snake resting at the base of the spine. As you shift your consciousness to the Kundalini, you'll feel the energy rising from the spine as if the snake were crawling up. The energy can flow freely up and down our spine until it reaches the crown of our body. The seventh Kundalini chakra, which is also the only chakra situated outside our physical body, is the final point Kundalini will flow through. This chakra, also known as Sahasrara, is the universal divine energy that requires a leap of faith from the yogi to achieve it. When the divine energy of our body coincides with the higher consciousness, Kundalini is said to be awakened. This spiritual awakening moves the being at its core and lights up every part of the body with radiant electric-like energy. An individual with an awakened Kundalini is deemed to be enlightened by the divine force of life.

What Enables Kundalini Awakening?

In today's world, experiencing Kundalini awakening is a rare thing. There are no ways to be certain of whether or not you'll be able to successfully awaken your Kundalini fully or when you'd be able to do it. Faith, belief, and karma have a lot to do with Kundalini awakening. People often experience a spontaneous awakening of the dormant energy in their bodies. However, the awakening that can transform the body, mind, and soul to a whole new level comes in its own time and at its own pace.

Primarily, there are two ways through which Kundalini can be awakened. The first route entails several years of dedication, hard work, and practice of the Kundalini yogic teachings and lifestyle. The second way happens through a spontaneous awakening which can be triggered even without training the mind or practicing for years. There's no way to know when or if the awakening will take place. It is believed that the spiritual journey of enlightenment begins well before we take a physical form in this world. That being said, it is also believed that your karma accumulated from this life, as well as your past lives, has a lot of impact on whether or not you're able to awaken the Kundalini. Dedication and practice are two things that can take us closer to our spiritual path.

1. Breathing Exercises

Those who consistently practice breathing techniques and can control their breath through exercises like pranayama can guide the energy to freely flow up and down their central core. Conscious control over breathing has been proven to enable the awakening of Kundalini.

2. Meditation

Meditation lies at the core of all yogic practices. Practicing meditation is a wonderful habit that can awaken the energies within the body. Rigorous sessions of meditation can act as a catalyst for Kundalini awakening.

3. Love

By opening the Anahata, or heart chakra, all emotional blockages can be discarded. The energy at the heart center enables a person to fall in love with oneself, others, and with all forms of life. Deep and true love is capable of helping with the process effectively and spontaneously.

4. Yoga Asanas

Performing yoga poses, or asanas, can clear the energy centers in our bodies. Specific yoga postures are also known to powerfully activate the Kundalini chakras. All types of yoga forms like Kundalini yoga and hatha yoga can trigger the awakening of Kundalini.

5. Prayers and Mantras

Prayers and chants emit vibrations of a certain frequency which can help break down the points of energy blockages. When we pray, there is a lot of intention involved. The dedication, motivation, and devotion to connecting with the higher consciousness can help trigger Kundalini awakening.

6. Spiritual Healing

All types of healing processes like Reiki healing, chakra opening, and psychological therapies are aimed at removing spiritual and mental blockages from the body. When the blockages are removed, Kundalini energy finds a way to flow freely through our core. The intent involved in energy healing can help with the Kundalini awakening.

7. Traumatic Experiences

Survival instincts are known to be one of the primal instincts that are naturally present in all living beings. Injury to the spine, depression, losing a loved one, physical separation, or near-death experiences can light up the survival instincts within us. The awakening of Kundalini energy can be triggered in an attempt to sustain life in life-threatening situations.

Effects and Signs of an Awakened Kundalini

The first thing to understand is that Kundalini energy is neither negative nor positive. It's a primordial form of energy that resides within all of us and, if harnessed correctly, can provide the chance for a better life. The symptoms and aftereffects that people experience through Kundalini yoga differ from one person to another. Since an experience depends on a person's karma, mindset, level of consciousness, energy blockages, and several other factors. The pleasantness or unpleasantness of the experience is completely subjective. However, several effects and symptoms are commonly experienced by those who practice Kundalini yoga.

1. Physical Effects

When the Kundalini is in the process of awakening, you may experience various physical symptoms like an intense rush of energy, chills, headaches, or even tingling sensations where your spine is. Feeling feverish, crying, or waking up at random hours of the night are also some of the physical symptoms of Kundalini awakening. People may also experience increased physical sensitivity and may feel compelled to make changes in their diet or sleep cycles. It is also common for people with an awakened Kundalini to experience a positive change in their immune systems.

A lot of physical changes can be attributed to the increased flow of energy in the nervous system of the body. Physical and energetic symptoms like visualizing things that aren't real, hearing music when none is playing, uncontrollable shaking, sudden bouts of energy, an inability to relax are all obvious signs of Kundalini awakening. The experience can be slow and stable for some people, while others may have intense and sudden experiences. One of the prime reasons for all the physical effects of Kundalini awakening can be the removal of energy blockages. When you practice Kundalini yoga, you may have the urge to dispose of all the self-held notions and destructive habits to enable an unobstructed flow of the Kundalini energy. Those who aren't prepared for the changes may find them to be overwhelming.

2. Mental Effects

Kundalini awakening can help you align your mindset and thoughts with a higher consciousness. Practicing Kundalini yoga can make you more attentive, conscious, and mentally sharp. Analyzing the problems or situations in one's life becomes a lot easier at this point. With an awakened Kundalini, the doors to leading a mindful life can open up. You start practicing mindfulness in every single act you do, be it eating, speaking, imagining, or breathing. It enables you to gleefully glide through stressful and happy situations alike.

By practicing Kundalini yoga, the amount of stress, anxiety, and pressure you experience in your current life can be dramatically reduced, which helps you assess any situation that you come across properly.

Kundalini awakening can also transform your perception of the outer world wherein the consequences of an act are visible to you even before they turn into reality. With the constant flow of divine energy within your system, you feel connected to yourself and to those around you. The awakening of Kundalini can dampen the ego, which may seem intimidating at first. However, once you realize that the ego is nothing but a collection of ideas in our minds that we weave about ourselves, the act of shedding it becomes much easier. You're freed from all the preconceived notions of life when your Kundalini is awakened.

3. Emotional Effects

In the process of Kundalini awakening, it is required to energize the heart chakra of the Kundalini. To remove any blockages that can disrupt the flow of the Kundalini energy, you may find yourself being confronted by strong emotional instances that happened in your past. In cases like these, a person may feel anxious, depressed, or experience feelings of despair. To experience Kundalini awakening, it is necessary to consciously accept the emotions and let them go.

It is common for people to see dramatic changes in their lives like changing jobs or partners because Kundalini awakening can make you leave everything behind that isn't aligned with your purpose. Once you're free of the emotional turmoil, you become more in tune with your feelings and emotions. You'll experience immense love and happiness in every moment that you're alive. You'll start paying more attention to your intuition and develop a deeper connection with yourself. The feelings of compassion and empathy are amplified, and they come naturally to you. When you're emotionally joyful, you feel more stable and connected with your soul and the nature of your true being. Kundalini awakening can increase the love you have for yourself, remove negative emotions, effectively enabling you to become your own healer.

4. Spiritual Effects

Dedication and devotion are one of the major factors that can enable Kundalini awakening. The belief in God, or a higher power, can lead to spiritual transformations in a human being. When you seek divine energy, it starts to manifest itself in your life. You'll find spending time outside in nature to be fulfilling and satisfying. Spirituality is a balance between devotion and service. Kundalini awakening can make you inclined to serve others. You start understanding, grasping, and applying the concept of "greater good" in all your thoughts, emotions, and actions. You'll find that serving others is the noblest and the most spiritual thing you can do with your life. An awakened Kundalini is believed to help you open and see through the third eye, or the inner eye. It helps you become acquainted with the true nature of yourself. That is, being connected with all forms of life force in this universe.

Dangers of Kundalini Awakening

Kundalini awakening can be an excellent tool for transforming your life's physical, emotional, mental, and spiritual aspects. It may be an effective way to heal and improve yourself, but without proper guidance, it poses several dangers to your health. Many Kundalini masters caution against attempting to forcefully induce a state of awakening. It must happen on its own accord when the body has been properly prepared for the transformation. When the central pathway is blocked, the premature rise of the Kundalini energy can cause mental and physical instability. It is easy to get side-tracked, disoriented, or overwhelmed if the awakening doesn't happen in a systematic and controlled manner.

Awakening the Kundalini requires clarity of thoughts, a silent mind, and clear intentions. Because it releases a tremendous force when awakened, practicing Kundalini yoga by yourself, without being knowledgeable about your practices, can be dangerous. You need to be careful of how you approach your Kundalini. There's a reason why it is depicted as a snake. If not handled with care and grace, it may become frightening and could very well poison your physical and mental health. As previously mentioned, when the layers of ego are being chipped away by the awakened Kundalini, the sudden loss of an element we were previously dependent on can cause a lot of discomfort. You must seek help from someone who's been through it if you wish to avoid an experience like this.

You must follow the correct processes like purification of self and do the necessary preparations to strengthen your core and mind before you can start activating the Kundalini chakras. This sacred art must be practiced in the presence of a trusted teacher or guru, who can guide you through the roller-coaster that is Kundalini awakening, at least for the first few times, until you find your bearings. Awakening the Kundalini can fill you up with a lot of energy. To understand how to manage this newly found power, you'll be needing a lot of support. A knowledgeable guru will help you process the sudden shift in perception that comes with the rise in Kundalini; otherwise, the experience can overwhelm you to a limit where you'll find yourself fearing the entire situation.

The process of Kundalini Awakening must never be rushed. A good teacher will know the safest and the best route for you to awaken your Kundalini. If you don't have proper guidance, spend time preparing yourself for the awakening and bring about conscious change in your lifestyle until you find a guru you can truly trust. You must be prepared to accept the shift in the dimensions of your life and ready to accommodate the immense power that Kundalini Awakening entails. Learn to take your time with everything, be kind to yourself, devote yourself to serving others, and embrace your life fully with love, care, and attention. With a stable mind, healthy body, dedicated work, strong intentions, and positive vibrations, you'll be able to embark on the journey of Kundalini Awakening and will eventually reach the shores of enlightenment.

Chapter 11: How to Support Your Kundalini Awakening

After learning about the process of Kundalini awakening and relevant signs that one develops along the way, this chapter will address coping mechanisms and techniques to deal with the symptoms that may arise. From getting mild headaches to developing depression or muscle spasms, the range of symptoms varies from mild to severe. The energy moves through your body and settles in different regions before it fully awakens. This can cause distress in major parts of the body and make the individual sick or uneasy due to the drastic change. Depending on the region and type of issue, one can treat and support the Kundalini awakening process relatively easily.

Why Can Kundalini Awakening Get Intense?

While some may experience a mild and blissful Kundalini awakening, most individuals go through a rough patch due to the overwhelming effect it has on the senses. Remember, once your Kundalini energy has been awakened, the way you employ your senses and react to the world around, will drastically change. As mentioned earlier, individuals going through the phenomenon of Kundalini awakening may experience light to heavy symptoms that can alter one's state and affect their overall well-being. Even though the energy supply is at a lower intensity or frequency, the effect may seem stronger if your body is not ready to adapt to the sudden change. Depending on the person's health condition and their ability to sustain stress, they may develop a range of symptoms. While some can endure difficult situations, others may feel extremely uncomfortable, even in mild situations.

Consider the release of Kundalini energy in your body to be the water pressure in a firefighter's hose. It can be a bit difficult to control in the beginning, but you will get used to handling that much force. In other words, your body will prepare itself to absorb and even support the flow of energy with precision. All you need is to be patient, courageous, and follow a personalized regimen of meditation and spiritual practices. Even though your body is doing its best to accommodate and support the process, it may lack certain abilities, which you must enhance.

In some cases, previous or childhood trauma can hinder the process if it is left untreated. If you haven't opened up about the trauma or failed to consult a therapist, your Kundalini awakening process can become cumbersome. While some may wake up to an awakened Kundalini, others may have to suffer from the hardship of the awakening process.

Supporting the Process of a Mild Kundalini Awakening

Low to mild symptoms of Kundalini awakening are felt when the energy disperses through the body and near its final destination point at the crown chakra. Even though it can take time, your head starts to feel heavier, and you can feel detached from the world. Life regressions, feelings of grandiosity, the inability to set energetic boundaries, feeling intolerant and warm, sensitivity to outside triggers, and constant mood swings are some mild and temporary symptoms you may experience. While some coping techniques can help reduce the negative effects, you must wait and let it pass.

Avoid Social Gatherings

If you are feeling cranky, agitated, and raw, avoid attending social gatherings and meeting new people to avoid snapping at them. It will not only affect your image but also amplify all the negative symptoms you are dealing with after awakening. More importantly, dealing with large crowds in such a vulnerable state can make one more anxious and confused. If you are facing difficulty coping with the existing signs, you should actively try to put your mind at ease by staying in quieter places and avoiding extra stress.

This does not mean that you should not reach out to your loved ones when you feel like talking. Since people can easily get anxious and depressed through this process, it is encouraged to lean on their loved ones and talk to experts. The key is to avoid crowded places such as grocery stores, shopping malls, and gatherings or events. If you do need to attend any event, find a spot with fewer people or stand under the shade to avoid feeling overwhelmed.

Keep Away from Vices

Avoid drinking alcohol or smoking cigarettes during the Kundalini awakening process, as it can increase anxiety and escalate fear. If you are unable to control your urges, seek help from your doctor. Substances like cannabis and other drugs can drastically affect your mind, and you could confuse the aftermath of its use with the symptoms of Kundalini awakening.

Focus on Your Diet

Eating clean is one of the most effective ways to keep your physical health in check and avoid major health problems. Since digestion can be a mild side effect during Kundalini awakening, switching to nutritious foods can help you cope. Typically, Kundalini affects your stomach when the energy reaches your abdomen. During those days, your body will resist solid food, and you may end up vomiting everything you eat. Switch to healthier and liquid-based sources of nutrition, such as soups and stews, to keep the functioning of your body intact.

Take multivitamin supplements to acquire your daily nutritional value. Some may feel nauseous due to the sudden and significant dietary changes, which is a sign of needing to alter your diet plan yet again. Eliminate any form of meat, dairy, and wheat sources from your diet plan and incorporate as many vegetables and fruits as you can. Sip on warm water infused with lemon and ginger to cleanse your digestive system. Needless to say, you need to drink as much water as you can throughout the day (at least 8 to 10 glasses). If you are still facing any form of stomach problems, seek help from a professional to modify your diet.

Avoid Communication with Negative Sources

Avoid meeting and keeping in contact with people who hurt you and give you pain, be it physical, mental or emotional. Whether it's a friend or a relative, you do not need this kind of toxicity in your life. Since you are already in pain due to the loud awakening process, you will not be able to handle any more energy, especially one with negative vibrations. Take time to focus on yourself. You can either stay alone or get support from a person who actually cares without judging you. Talk to people who make you feel at ease and are there for you during harsh circumstances.

By negative sources, we don't just mean toxic people; toxic media, news sources, and other entities that can elevate the distress should all be avoided. If you are not satisfied with your job and are unhappy due to constant negative energy being thrown at you, take a break, or quit if you can. Be yourself; you don't have to prove anything to anyone. Shun yourself from all kinds of negativity and focus on positive matters. Take the time to rediscover yourself while your Kundalini is awakening. Nurture yourself by painting, reading, writing, drawing, dancing, or performing any other activity that cleanses your soul and puts your mind at ease.

Do Not Listen to Spiritual Stories

If you want to treat your anxiety, switch to mindful practices instead of listening to spiritual stories. Simple tactics like sipping on soothing tea, performing yoga, and meditating can also help. Journaling is known to be an effective way to treat anxiety. Maintain a bullet journal and jot down your thoughts (not just the happy ones, but also those that scare or haunt you). With this, you can face your fears and gather courage. Practice gratitude and thank the universe for the things you are blessed with and are grateful for. Taking relaxing baths and listening to calming music are dainty ways to stay calm and treat anxiety as well. Try aromatherapy by diffusing essential oils around you. Certain essential oils like chamomile, lavender, and citrus can calm your senses and alleviate stress-inducing symptoms.

Supporting an Intense Kundalini Awakening

As mentioned, most individuals undergo a rigorous Kundalini awakening process that can increase anxiety and fear. However, there are several ways to support and alleviate pertinent signs. The experiences when undergoing this process are often compared to the symptoms of someone entering puberty. Even though both processes are irrelevant to each other, adults may feel like they are going through the process of puberty and adolescence once again, as an awakened Kundalini describes a now matured soul. In most cases, teenagers feel agitated and suffer from various physical changes due to hormonal imbalance. Since they are unaware of the process, they can take time to adjust to the new changes. Similarly, adults going through Kundalini awakening can be perplexed. Consider this when faced with a conundrum like this.

Avoid Practicing Healing Techniques

Healing practices like acupuncture and Reiki should be avoided during Kundalini awakening, especially if the symptoms are severe. Only when you are far from seeking Kundalini awakening will you be able to practice any form of healing techniques. Since individuals experiencing this are already sensitive (and even over-sensitive in some cases), a simple healing process can aggravate symptoms, some of which may not even be present in the first place. For instance, you cannot expect an energy healer to repel your sexual desires during puberty; similarly, the energizing feeling during Kundalini awakening cannot be healed with Reiki or similar practices. Kundalini, just like a person's libido, cannot be remodeled by any living being or energy source, thereby making these efforts useless.

This is particularly important if you are not good at performing any healing exercises. Doing it incorrectly can aggravate the signs and make the situation much worse. Yogic breathing, re-birthing, and other breathing exercises should also be avoided, as they can impact the mind and soul. Before you know it, certain disastrous repercussions may affect your health. Handle this as you would prescription drugs; they should not be consumed unless advised by an experienced practitioner.

Avoid Reading Negative Stories

Needless to say, you should avoid reading negative stories related to Kundalini awakening. You are already scared, worried, or anxious due to the agonizing process; reading someone else's story can further overwhelm you and produce hesitation. Stay away from the internet as it is filled with terrifying and often untrue stories of people undergoing their Kundalini awakening. Even if you are facing mild symptoms, reading these stories can activate the placebo effect, which can worsen your condition. Although the chances of circumstances like these occurring are far less than the alternative.

Instead, divert your attention to the positive effects of the process and think about the positive changes you will feel once your Kundalini has been fully awakened. Gathering multiple sources of Kundalini awakening is also not advised, as you may come across stories that you must avoid reading or hearing about.

Live a Peaceful and Wholesome Life

Try to live as peacefully and fruitfully as you can. Focus on your physical and mental health. Make peace with others around you and keep away from negativity. Discard anything upsetting in your life- alcohol, drugs, toxic relationships, etc. Develop and maintain a spiritual outlook to stay closer to the higher power and unravel the mystical dimension that is invisible to us. Do not get attached to material possessions and live a simple and content life.

Build trust, but do not rely fully on others. Be as independent as you can to lead a peaceful and wholesome life. However, you must not overindulge in spiritual activities as they can exaggerate the energy flow process throughout the body. This can worsen your condition and cause an imbalance. If you are new to this process, seek help from a spiritual guru or meditation teacher to teach you to establish the proper balance for you. Schedule your daily activities to accommodate a few minutes of meditation and learn the correct method from your guru.

Gain Power

You need the power to face the overwhelming emotions of the process. When going through Kundalini awakening, an individual unconsciously gains the power to resist the force and maintain their stance. It is similar to the power that people gain during puberty to develop their organs and prepare the body to create a new living being. Similarly, some forms of power, like supernatural abilities, clairvoyance, telepathy, etc., are unconsciously developed by humans during Kundalini awakening.

While some gain these powers without doing much work, others need to cultivate them through certain practices. Bringing radical changes to your life and body can accelerate the process and bring you closer to the power. Most of the changes will not be forced. Just like you grow due to different phases in your life- turning a simple attraction into a long-term relationship, becoming a parent, and becoming more responsible, the challenges you take up during your Kundalini awakening process can turn you into a new person and teach you new lessons.

Seek Help from a Personal Guide

A spiritual guide can support you throughout the journey and direct you on the right path. Since they are familiar with the intensity of Kundalini and its awakening process, they can guide you with diligence. They can also validate your condition during the process without judging you. It is highly likely that they have been through a similar journey. Hence, gaining insights and motivation from an expert is worth the time and effort. Basically, you need a good support system that can help without shaming you and keeping the information inaccessible.

If possible, get in touch with an awakened mentor as they are fully aware of their surroundings and can provide detailed insights related to your process. They will sit with you when you meditate and will help bring peace into your life. They will also teach you the true meaning of compassion and tolerance, which is also one of the goals of Kundalini awakening. You will constantly have someone who understands your thoughts and emotions, thereby simplifying the process and promoting a fresh outlook on life. Since the process and symptoms vary from one person to another, you may face extremely personal and rare thoughts and incidents that not many can understand or relate to. However, since your spiritual guru has been through this process already, they can offer valuable insights on how to deal with situations like these.

Handling Kundalini Awakening Based on the Symptoms

Those forced to deal with a collection of symptoms during the process of Kundalini awakening may face ambiguity and confusion. Certain expressions may suddenly seem extremely strange, which can make coping with them extremely difficult. They can neither be categorized as mild symptoms nor as heavy signs. Even though you may be able to deal with these issues with time, you must try certain coping mechanisms to develop insights and wisdom to sustain the arduous journey and persevere throughout. Let's take a look at some "strange" signs and bizarre experiences, along with relevant coping mechanisms to handle Kundalini awakening.

Blissful or Psychic Experiences

If you experience bliss or see psychic visions, be patient and allow the moments to pass on their own. While you can easily endure bliss and enjoy every moment of it, certain negative visions can be a bit difficult to deal with. Know that both stages will pass, and you will eventually make peace with them. Note that it is easy to get attached to blissful experiences. If you do get attached, rebounding to your previous state becomes a possibility. The best thing to do is to experience, withstand, and avoid getting attached. Whether it's good or bad, remember that every moment will pass.

Psychics suggest that experiencing bliss is similar to the "honeymoon" phase; the individual revels in the novelty of their new being before they face reality. The real relationship that commences later is harder to endure, which is similar to the Kundalini awakening process. It starts with mild strength and can get ferocious at certain times. The only way to handle these situations is to stay patient and calm. The visions and insights you gain during the process should be remembered, as they can be valuable to you in the future.

Spontaneous Shaking or Involuntary Movements

The process of energy flow may cause involuntary shaking or spontaneous movements due to the body's inability to handle the new source of energy. These jitters or trembles are known as "kriyas" in Sanskrit. This is a coping mechanism by your body to get rid of the excess energy it receives. It is similar to shivering when we are cold as the body attempts to regulate the temperature inside and around it. This is also experienced through muscle spasms or seizures in extreme cases.

While most kriyas can be controlled through willpower, some may be difficult to control. This can cause anxiety or even force you to stay isolated. The best way to deal with kriyas is to stay still and shift your path of consciousness through meditation. This will not only mellow the involuntary movements but also give you more confidence to no longer isolate yourself from the world after your transition. If the kriyas keep returning, you can train your muscles to deal with the jitters. With time, you will be comfortable and confident enough to let the kriyas pass just through sheer willpower.

Feeling Anxious or Scared

Feeling anxious and scared is also common when faced with an overflow of energy. If you are already worried about your personal and professional life, the intense process of Kundalini awakening and relevant signs can make one more anxious. The idea is to activate your parasympathetic nervous system through activities that you enjoy. For example, you can resort to dancing, playing an instrument, creating art, or singing. Treating anxiety is of utmost importance, as prolonged signs can negate the positive effects of Kundalini. You can also try breathing techniques or take anti-anxiety pills for extreme cases.

Most people voluntarily practice certain postures to divert the energy coming their way and balance their chakras. This can also be practiced when your surroundings are filled with negative energy and you wish to get rid of it. Take around 15 to 30 minutes daily and practice postures when you feel that your energy levels become imbalanced. It becomes even more crucial when you start feeling a throbbing pain in your head or crown chakra due to the overflow of energy.

Nihilism and Lucid Dreams

To add to the list of negative symptoms, you may feel empty or lose interest in life. Following the principle of nihilism is extremely uncommon and is often related to a lack of empathy or emotions. If you prefer being social, make sure to set boundaries to avoid triggering others around you. Instead, focus on self-care and work on being compassionate again. Know that you are sensitive, acknowledge your situation, and try to be kind to yourself and others. Look for inspiration around you, try to be creative, and practice mindfulness to gain your former perspective of "the meaning of life".

Experiencing lucid dreams is another common sign that occurs in people going through the last phase of Kundalini awakening. Lucid dreams can be intimidating and may leave a mark on your mind. The best way to cope with this is to maintain a dream journal and note all your weird or fascinating dreams in it. Once you are able to decipher the pattern of your dreams, you will be able to handle them more efficiently and face your fears before going to bed.

Physical Health Conditions

As you learned, it is common to develop certain physical health conditions such as digestive issues, insomnia, eating disorders that result in extreme weight gain or loss, autoimmune diseases, or skin conditions. The simplest way to take care of your physical health is by eating cleaner and exercising on a regular basis. If you gain or lose a major amount of weight in a short period, be patient and note that the situation is temporary. With the changed diet plan, you will be able to return to your normal weight in no time. It will also help you deal with eating disorders if you have developed any due to Kundalini awakening.

Sleep disorders or insomnia can be cured by exercising regularly and tiring your body. If it doesn't work, talk to a therapist or take sleeping pills after consulting your medical practitioner. To treat muscle pain or soreness, get a massage or take a hot shower. Approaching a holistic doctor can help you diagnose and treat autoimmune conditions. Most importantly, rest and relax; note that this situation of feeling irregular is temporary, and it will pass in no time.

If you are feeling fuzzy, confused, agitated, or depressed due to the process, try to reshape or shift your perception to feel at ease. It can help mellow down fear and give you more courage to face any situation. The key is to recognize the signs and treat them one at a time. Carry this process with patience and a steady mind. Do not panic if things seem confusing, and seek help if necessary. As mentioned, appoint a spiritual guide and consult your medical practitioner to treat spiritual and physical symptoms, respectively. Lean on your loved ones when you face the overwhelming effect of Kundalini awakening.

Chapter 12: The Third Eye and Third Eye Opening

The third eye, or Ajna chakra, is believed to be the hidden sixth sense. It represents intelligence, intuition, psychic ability, and wisdom. Upon awakening your third eye, you can "sense" the vibrations and achieve visions that are closely connected to your spirit. In other words, it can help you descry your behavioral, spiritual, and psychological characteristics on a deeper level. You can achieve a state of balance and a sense of freedom with an active Ajna chakra. One's nervous system, eyes, and sinuses are monitored and balanced by the third eye.

The Relation between Third Eye and Kundalini Awakening

Even though the opening of the Third Eye and Kundalini awakening are deemed independent processes, they are obscurely related. Many argue that the third eye or Ajna chakra is not related to Kundalini, as both can be active or inactive, irrespective of the other's condition. While Kundalini provides and pushes the flow of positive energy throughout one's body, the third eye provides spiritual sight. Even though both events should be independent of each other, they become inseparable once a higher level is reached. In simpler words, you need to infuse Kundalini energy to accelerate the process of the third eye activation.

By opening or activating the third eye, you can "see" clearly and perceive reality with a higher purpose. Your physical and spiritual realm will seem closer and clearer, which is also one of the main goals of Kundalini Awakening.

The Ajna Chakra

Discovering various aspects of the Ajna chakra can help you understand its significance and explore it in depth.

Yogic Significance

The Ajna Chakra or the Third Eye is recognized using several names, such as brow chakra, Dvidak Padma, and Bhru Madhya. Psychics and yoga enthusiasts commonly refer to this point as Ajna chakra, which translates to "perceive" or "command" in Sanskrit. All the pure elements, when combined, exert an intense force, which thereby relates to the Third Eye or the "supreme element". In other words, transcending the duality that separates your true character from the outer world can be accomplished by opening the third eye. This is also known as I-consciousness, wherein your "I" characteristic disintegrates from the rest of the world and continues to exist apart from the rest of the world.

In essence, a yogi seeking "Mukti" (freedom from the existential world) often looks into transcending through all the chakras and the five elements that connect one's mind, body, and soul to the universe. We are bound to time and reality, which define our consciousness. When you succeed in transcending the Vishuddha Chakra (located at the throat region), you can move on to the process of awakening the Ajna Chakra, which is a definite way to move from I-consciousness to super-consciousness.

Location

The third eye is located in the center of both eyebrows on the forehead. This unique point is known for its powerful foresight and intuitive force. With an open third eye, one can drive their imaginative power to its utmost creativity and openness. Many assume that the third eye is located in the middle of the forehead, which is a common misconception. Spot the center of your eyebrows and place your finger slightly above your nose bridge to find the exact location of your third eye. The middle of the forehead, where many believe the third eye to be, actually houses some secondary chakras, which are intricately connected to the Ajna chakra (despite being situated a bit lower).

Our pineal gland, which is located in the brain, regulates the sleep and wake cycle. In other words, it is responsible for monitoring and regulating the biorhythms of one's body. The various states of consciousness are often mystical and alter our center of attention (which is regulated by the pineal gland) due to the way our eyes and brain perceive light and connect it to reality. The optical nerves are closely connected to the pineal gland, which increases its sensitivity to visually stimulating elements. Any kind of lighting change can also increase sensitivity.

Symbols and Colors

The lotus flower and the upside-down triangle are two intricate symbols representing the third eye. Since both symbols represent wisdom, they are highly suitable to denote the Ajna chakra.

The color of Ajna chakra is represented by a bluish-purple hue. The energy of the third eye, when perceived in an auric state, can be perceived as bluish-white or translucent purple. While the color helps you recognize the state of your aura, your third eye should be perceived through the quality of luminescence it spreads. The soft radiance emitted from the auric energy also resembles moonlight. Usually, strong shades of indigo or a mix of violet and dark blue can be used to represent the Ajna chakra.

Behavioral Characteristics

The reason why most people are interested in obtaining psychic qualities through Kundalini yoga in an attempt to awaken their third eye is that it transports you to the inconspicuous dimension that exists separately from our perceived reality. You get to see the subtle qualities that the third eye chakra exposes you to. Let's take a wide look at the behavioral, psychological, and spiritual characteristics that the third eye imposes.

Vision

The way you see and perceive the world becomes entirely different and fascinating when you succeed in opening the third eye. The images you form in your head may also be difficult to describe. In other words, the intangible visuals are easily grasped by the mind yet hard to formulate in human words. As compared to regular visions, the ones seen through the third eye are more ineffable and subtle. At times, they may seem dreamy or blurry, but if you perceive the visuals with your inner eye, you may be able to screen them more clearly than your actual vision that observes reality.

Basically, it is like a movie with incomprehensible illustrations that run through your mind. In some cases, individuals have reported having seen vague storyboards that they later experienced. You can call these psychic visions, which act as a sixth sense and help you alter intense situations that may occur in the future.

Intuition

The visions and illustrations you discern through your third eye strengthen your intuition as well. As mentioned, the sixth sense intensifies with the awakening of the third eye, which improves your intuitive power and keeps you away from danger.

Knowledge

An individual with an active third eye is perceived as an intellectual person and becomes highly regarded within their discipline. With an active third eye, you get to explore different dimensions of reality, which can enhance your wisdom.

Spiritual and Psychological Functions

When your third eye awakens and is stimulated, it connects to the realm of spirits and archetypal dimensions, which affect your mind and soul at a greater level. Some of the spiritual and psychological effects or benefits are clairvoyance (special sight) and clairaudience (enhanced sense of hearing), the ability to access the mystical states, inspiration, creativity, and gaining wisdom and valuable insights.

Imbalance in the Third Eye

Any kind of imbalance caused in the third eye chakra can affect your personal and professional life greater than you'd expect. This can be due to some form of energy blockages or habits that hamper your vitality. In other words, it can disorient your perception of reality and put you in psychic distress. If not treated, it can break the efficacy of your energy system. Here are signs or effects of imbalance in your third eye chakra.

Feeling Lost or Ill

You may feel lost and stuck in the sluggish, monotonous pattern that tends to bind you to a tight schedule every day. It can be brought on by your work, your thoughts, or your relationship. Your problems and issues may feel like a big burden that you find very difficult to overcome. In extreme cases, energy blocks can also result in sickness or deadly illnesses. You may feel dull, restless, weak, and exhausted.

The Inability to Perceive Your Goals

When your third is inactive or overactive (or, in other words, imbalanced), your mind will either feel empty (resulting in a lack of clarity) or feel exhausted due to the rushing thoughts. It is common to constantly feel overwhelmed with an overactive third eye. Apart from the inability to perceive your goals, you may also lack focus and have clouded judgment. Nausea, seizures, vision issues, headaches, and anxiety attacks are also some of the commonly observed physical symptoms that arise due to third eye chakra blockages.

Psychic Fantasies

Your body's entire chakra system should balance each other out and stabilize the functioning of each arrangement that is responsible for your overall well-being. While an inactive Ajna chakra can undeniably be a problem, an overactive third eye can cause an imbalance too. In these cases, your mind will illustrate illusions that seem fantasy-like and far away from reality. These delusions can create expectations that may not be fulfilled in the future. While a balanced Ajna chakra helps you face reality in an alternate dimension (which can be beneficial for your well-being), an overactive third eye can push you into a whirlwind of indulgence. In the long run, this can result in greed and vices.

An overactive third eye can push you into a downward spiral and create phantasmagoric visions that can lead you to believe false bits of information. Furthermore, if you are not grounded, you may overindulge in vices and immerse yourself in the fantasy world your third eye has created for itself. Pulling back can be very difficult at this point. The difference is, in action, this third eye lets you differentiate between your imagination and reality, and so you make sane choices. However, an overactive sixth sense chakra fails to draw the line and drives you to believe your imagination to be reality.

Rejection

An imbalanced or inactive third eye can result in feelings of rejection and hatred. Whether or not you excel at your work and relationships, you may constantly feel rejected by some person or entity in your personal and professional spheres.

This can also affect you at a spiritual level. The feeling of not being able to connect to your soul and feeling scared when facing your thoughts is also common. Everything that is beyond the spiritual level will undeniably seem too far-fetched.

Lack of Focus

You may face a lack of guiding vision that obstructs your ability to focus and eats away at your concentration levels. This, in turn, can result in decreased productivity, pushing you further away from reaching your goals. These pit stops can seriously affect your career and regress your professional and personal growth. If this continues, you may also fail to see the bigger picture and where you are currently heading. The lack of clarity and inability to design your final goals will accompany this phenomenon. Before it's too late, you should construct a vision for yourself and adapt accordingly. You must cipher the path you are currently on and decide your next step to excel.

How to Activate the Third Eye

At times, certain imbalances in your body's chakra systems can also affect your vision, perception, and imaginative power. This takes place when you practice or invite habits that sabotage your energy. These energetic blocks need to be discarded as soon as possible. In this section, we will overview effective ways for you to access your vitality and activate the third eye to unleash your inner being's true potential.

Yoga Kriyas

Certain kriyas or yoga asanas can enhance a person's ability to perceive the world with a heightened sense. This, in turn, can help them awaken their third eye and explore life with sheer transparency. In fact, two of the most powerful ways to activate the sixth chakra are yoga and meditation. It is believed that the imbalance in one's third eye is not just due to the inactivity of the sixth chakra system but an overall imbalance in the entire body. By balancing the rest of the chakras, you can safeguard the Ajna chakra as well. This is when Kundalini yoga kriya can help you.

The yoga kriyas or asanas you perform translate to "seated posture" in the Sanskrit language. Here are yoga poses you can try to activate your third eye. You will need a yoga mat and a silent and safe space.

Child's Pose (Balasana)

One of the most effective asanas to strengthen and elongate the spine, Child's Pose is a popular posture among yoga enthusiasts. It offers a stimulating and energizing feeling, which is why it can be performed as a counter asana. Since it lets you focus in an inward position, you can perform this asana to open the Ajna chakra.

How to Perform It: Sit on the floor with your legs tucked under you and your hips resting comfortably on your heels. Keep your back and torso straight. Slowly bend your upper body and lean forward while extending your arms in front of you. Try to touch the floor with your nose or forehead while keeping your hands straight above you. Take deep breaths and stay in this position for a few minutes.

Downward-Facing Dog (Adho Mukha Svanasana)

Apart from calming your sixth chakra, this asana also helps relax your mind and stretches your calves. The forward bending pose is also known to provide a stimulating effect to your whole body.

How to Perform It: Begin by getting on all fours with your wrists underneath your shoulders and your knees hip-width apart. Curl your toes under your feet and lift your knees off the ground. Simultaneously, splay your fingers on the mat and push your hips back to raise your rump to the ceiling to form an inverted V-shape with your body. Your ears should be beside your shoulders. Take deep breaths and hold this position for a while. Exhale and slowly release the position.

Standing Half Forward Bend (Ardha Uttanasana)

One of the most cogent methods to improve your lower back strength, performing this asana can also send a gush of energy flowing through your Ajna chakra. This, in turn, can activate your sixth sense.

How to Perform It: Stand up straight with your legs at hip-width apart. While keeping a straight back, tighten your torso and bend your upper body forward so that it is parallel to the floor. Keep the knees and feet straight. Plant your feet firmly on the ground to maintain the position. Extend your arms so that your fingers touch the floor. Keep your gaze on the floor to avoid straining your neck and hold this position for a few minutes. Inhale deeply and slowly lift your torso to release this position.

Since this pose can intensely utilize your back muscles, consult your doctor before including this asana in your regime, especially if you have a lower back issue.

Supported Shoulder Stand (Salamba Sarvangasana)

This inverted pose stretches your limbs, neck, and shoulders and helps with calming your mind and the sixth chakra.

How to Perform It: Lie down on the floor and keep your arms and legs straight. Inhale and exhale at a continuous pace. Place your legs together and lift them while keeping your back firmly on the floor. Extend your legs towards the ceiling so that they are perpendicular to the floor. Keep your knees straight, and your hands rested on the floor. Until you improve, slightly lean your legs back to slowly lift your lower back off the ground and use your hands for support in order to keep your legs extended upwards. Your elbows should be resting on the mat, and your forearms should be perpendicular to it. Keep your upper back, neck, and head on the floor. Hold this position for a few seconds or minutes. Initially, it may seem a bit difficult, but you can steadily increase the time and practice holding the position for a few minutes at a stretch.

Hero (Virasana)

As compared to other asanas, this posture is relatively easier and highly effective, which makes it a highly recommended addition to your yoga regime. You can perform this asana in a seated position to strengthen your lower body. Utilizing your knees and ankles, this asana also treats your digestive issues and cleanses your sixth chakra system.

How to Perform It: Sit on the floor by folding at the knees and lucking your legs under your hips. Now, gradually push your lower legs outwards, so your hips are resting just beside your heels, and your toes should face outwards. Place your palms on your knees and straighten your back to lengthen your spine. Close your eyes and stay in this position for a few minutes while taking deep breaths.

Big Toe (Padangusthasana)

Along with strengthening your calves and hamstrings, use this pose consistently to open your sixth chakra system.

How to Perform It: Stand straight with your legs parallel with 6-inches of the distance between them. Keeping your upper body straight, slowly bend forward and tuck your fingers under your toes. If you can, try to touch your forehead to your knees. Make sure not to strain yourself. Inhale and exhale while staying in this position for a few minutes. Inhale deeply and slowly lift your torso to release this position.

Needless to say, performing yoga on a regular basis is not just necessary to activate your Ajna chakra but also to maintain your physical health.

Meditation

Meditation is the easiest and most effective way to face your thoughts and fears. This practice helps you engage with your soul and spirit, which then makes you more aware and active as a person. Meditation is also useful in activating your third eye if practiced the right way. Sit in a quiet room and listen to music that resonates at 720 Hz. Just like every chakra vibrates and aligns to a different frequency, the sixth chakra system steadily activates at this range. Singing bowls, tuning forks, and certain musical instruments can be used to produce this sound effect. You can also try meditation breathing techniques to feel an energetic force in the center of your eyes.

Seek Help from Your Dreams

The dreams and visions you get when sleeping can be used to activate your third eye. Not many know this, but your dreams convey the thoughts of your inner voice. Your mind and soul seek an astral journey when you are asleep. The visions and illusions often go unnoticed as you tend to forget most of the dreams and visions you experience through a REM cycle. Whether positive or negative, any kind of dream you see, especially a recurring one, should not be dismissed. Keep a dream journal to mark the pattern of your dreams and decipher them to hear your inner voice and stimulate your sixth sense.

Use Healing Crystals

Certain crystals are solely meant for or are highly effective at activating the third eye because they are packed with energetic vibrations that can spread positivity and balance the sixth sense chakra. Since the Ajna chakra is represented by indigo, purple, and dark blue hues, you can use crystals that have similar shades. Some of them are Dumortierite, Azurite, Lapis Lazuli, Labradorite, and Sodalite. The positive vibrations of these crystals can relieve mental stress, calm your mind, and strengthen your intuitive power. In a way, these crystals work to balance and activate your Ajna chakra.

You can either hold them when meditating, wear them as a necklace pendant, or place them beside your bed or desk. When using crystals, you must ensure that they are recharged from time to time. Crystals with low or dull energy will fail to provide the results you are looking for. Scrutinize the properties of the crystals you are using to determine the most effective way of recharging them. Some common ways are placing them under the moonlight or submerging them in saltwater.

Third Eye Affirmations

You can repeat certain affirmations or positive statements when practicing rituals to awaken your third eye. The power of positivity and attraction are relatable when activating chakras and trying to balance them. The best part is, this practice is extremely easy and takes just a few times in order for it to become effective. Moreover, you can practice it without any time or space constraints.

Here are sentences you can repeat to yourself when performing asanas or simply looking in the mirror.

- I trust my gut and intuition.
- I am fairly connected to my spiritual realm.
- I can connect to the higher power.
- My intuition is strong.

- My soul is guiding me on the right path.

- I am growing and learning with time.

- I can see and design the bigger picture.

- My imagination is powerful.

- I can connect to my true self.

- My inner wisdom is leading me.

- I am steadily turning into my best version.

Apart from these beneficial ways to activate and balance the sixth chakra system, you should also focus on consuming a clean and nutritious diet. The food you consume can majorly impact your body's chakra system, which, in turn, can affect the activity of your third eye. You can also incorporate aromatherapy, sound therapy, and Reiki in your wellness regime (we will talk more about this in the next chapter).

By following these methods, you can actively address the energy blocks that are hindering your third eye. In a way, practicing Kundalini yoga can optimize and stimulate your energy system to activate your Ajna chakra and unleash its power.

Chapter 13: Reiki Healing and Its Relation to Awakening

Reiki refers to an energy source that is guided by one's spirit. A Reiki master heals one's suffering by transferring positive energy from their body onto the afflicted. It is usually done by laying hands on the other person's body or by chanting prayers. Reiki has existed since the 1800s and was first used in Japan. In fact, the word "Reiki" is an amalgamation of two Japanese words, "Rei" meaning higher power and "Ki" meaning the force or energy of life.

In a way, Reiki helps us meet our authentic self through physical, mental, and spiritual healing. Reiki uses distinct levels of attunements by reaching into one's chakras and opening them up. A Reiki master summons the universe's energy and acts as a medium to send positive vibrations into a living being. Almost every individual practicing Reiki has experienced some form of its positive effect. Let's take a look at the practice of Reiki and its relation to Kundalini awakening in-depth.

How is Kundalini Awakening Related to Reiki Healing?

While Reiki is predominantly used to energize one's body and send it positive vibrations, it can also be used to aid in the awakening of Kundalini energy. This healing process is known as Kundalini Reiki and is steadily gaining traction within the domain of yoga. Even though the technique produces positive effects, it is devoid of any complexity. The straightforward approach and instant benefits make Kundalini Reiki even more intriguing. The concept of Kundalini Reiki was first anointed by the master of meditation, Ole Gabrielsen. Essentially, this process acts on the blocks and knots that one might have in their chakras, which can block the flow of positive energy throughout the body.

Furthermore, Kundalini Reiki also recognizes the soul's model or blueprint and acts according to the individual's desires. Since the process of awakening one's Kundalini can be a rigorous process, taking help from Reiki is an efficient, safe, and quick way to accelerate energy flow within the body. When practicing Kundalini Reiki, you must go through a detailed yet simple attunement process that opens and heals your chakras. In turn, it opens up a channel that enables your body to receive the energy. This induces a healing process that calms your senses and treats signs of physical and mental illness.

A common belief is that a person's consciousness and inner being are developed through the successful release of Kundalini energy. The process starts from the crown chakra and continues down to the base of the spine. The Kundalini energy then stays there until the person exerts efforts to awaken it. Unconsciously, every person wishes for their Kundalini to wake up and travel to where it originated from, namely the crown chakra. While Kundalini provides the strength and energy to feel enlightenment, Reiki makes one more aware of their potential and consciousness. When combined, both forms turn into a healing modality. You can mold your desires, transform your life, and form a deep connection with your soul. You are not only clearer about your goals and ultimate purpose in life but are also capable of finding answers to achieve them.

In essence, Kundalini can be defined as an individual's true self that is veiled by their visible attributes. One's divine self is often difficult to unravel, which is where Reiki steps in. It helps an individual dig deeper and unveil their true self. Even though they are separate domains, they are substantially similar. Both our divine self and true self are symbiotically connected and are brought into unison by the combination of Kundalini and Reiki. The esoteric traditions of Japan associate Reiki with the dragon symbol, and as you know, Kundalini is represented by the snake symbol in Indian tradition. In Sanskrit, the word "Naga" represents the dragon and snake, which further displays that both forms are intricately connected.

To complete a course of Kundalini Reiki, you must go through three attunements, which can take up to 10 days. While the first attunement must be undertaken with a Reiki master present, the other two can be practiced alone. Rituals like practicing self-healing, understanding karmic bands, healing over a distance, healing qualities, and cleansing a room are taught during the first attunement. The other two comprise Kundalini Reiki healing and self-healing, internal cleansing, and regular meditation. From gathering insights and consciousness to manifest positive changes in life to gaining courage and flexibility, Kundalini Reiki can benefit an individual on many different levels.

Is Reiki Effective?

Some experts claim that Reiki works due to the placebo effect, where the patient feels more energized and positive because they deeply believe in the healing properties of Reiki. Despite this pretense, the healing benefits due to the "universe's vibrations" are known to show positive effects, and the non-invasive nature of the procedure makes Reiki one of the most sought-after healing methods today. Even though Reiki is often scoffed at and perceived as nothing if not pseudoscience, its healing properties and practical benefits are compelling the medical world to open its eyes and recognize this practice for what it is.

Health Benefits of Reiki

Needless to say, Reiki offers numerous health benefits. From energizing your mind and body to treating minute issues that affect your physical health, Reiki offers a myriad of advantages.

Reduces Stress and Enhances Mood

Reiki is known to reduce stress through its positive vibrations. A single session of Reiki enhances your mood and induces a relaxing effect, which, in turn, can put you at ease. A scientific study showed that people who went through stressful situations while partaking in Reiki sessions felt lighter and more relaxed than those who didn't. It is believed that undergoing just six 30-minute sessions of Reiki can have a visible effect on one's mood and reduce stress by a greater margin. It can make you feel happier and give you more power to deal with stressful situations.

Treats Depression

Individuals claim to feel "happier" just after one session of Reiki and can finish an entire course to actively alleviate signs of depression. This can be particularly useful for the elderly who particularly have a hard time-fighting depression. The inability to complete tasks on time, social isolation, and unnecessary fear are signs of depression. In extreme cases, a depressed person is highly likely to commit suicide as well. Whether it's a mild or intense case of depression, seek help from Reiki to improve your overall mental health or as part of your self-care regimen.

Reduces Signs of Anxiety and Pain

Reiki works directly on the parasympathetic nervous system, which effectively alleviates signs of depression, pain, and anxiety. It also regulates blood pressure and heart rate, which is beneficial for individuals with cardiovascular or heart issues. Patients diagnosed with cancer or other serious health issues often have increased levels of anxiety. They fear seeking treatment due to the possible side effects of the medication. Due to this, medical practitioners are advising patients to seek Reiki and other non-invasive treatments that can help them feel calmer and control symptoms related to anxiety. Women undergoing labor and painful cramps can seek help from Reiki and reduce the dependence on analgesic painkillers.

May Treat Headache and Insomnia

Those suffering from headaches, nausea, or insomnia on a regular basis can also seek help from Reiki. Sleeping disorders and headaches often happen due to increased stress. As you know, Reiki can alleviate symptoms caused by stress, which may treat headaches and help you sleep. Along with this, Reiki is also known to treat herniated disks and lower back pains. Other health issues such as nausea and hypertension can also be reduced with Reiki. It all boils down to the relaxing feeling offered by consistently engaging in Reiki sessions.

Improves Quality of Life

In general, Reiki is known to improve the quality of life and make it more manageable. Whether it's your physique, mental health issues, or personal problems that are deteriorating the quality of your life, you can turn towards Reiki. If done consistently, having sessions with Reiki masters can help people find opportunities, partners and even help with fertility issues. The masters prepare their candidates for these constructive future events by sending positive vibrations into their bodies and around them. Apart from preparing for the future, Reiki can also help heal the traumatic or sad experiences of the past. If you are having trouble moving on from the past, you should definitely give Reiki a shot.

How Is Reiki Carried Out?

A typical Reiki session may take a few minutes to a couple of hours, depending on the intensity of the situation. Your Reiki master will lead you to a silent room and ask you to lie on a table or sit on the floor in a comfortable position. Depending on your preference, the Reiki master may play calming music. During the healing process, the Reiki master will spot specific areas of your hands, head, torso, and limbs. They will monitor you and place their hands on the affected areas using different positions. This can take up to 5 or 10 minutes. The teacher can spot and place their hands on 20 different spots. If you are injured or feel pain when touched on a certain body part, the master will hover their hand over the spot and conduct begin the Reiki process. At this point, Reiki masters usually close their eyes and say prayers or chant mantras to send positive energy into your body. Once the spot feels warm and springs a tingling sensation, the master will move on to the next spot. They usually feel the energy abating from their end, which is when they confirm that the energy has been successfully transmitted into your body. As mentioned, the session can take up to 90 minutes or 2 hours, depending on your needs.

You can also practice Reiki at home. According to expert Reiki masters, follow these steps when performing Reiki on yourself.

Step 1: Find a sustainable and comfortable posture. The best way is to sit cross-legged (lotus pose or Padmasana). You can also lie down and use bolsters to support your joints.

Step 2: Understand and know your intentions. Why did you consider practicing Reiki on your own? How did you manage to take time out? Honor and validate your intentions to discard intimidation and practice Reiki with courage.

Step 3: Take deep breaths and meditate. You must feel relaxed and remove any fears before practicing Reiki. Next, you will recite Reiki precepts to cleanse your mind and soul. Effective precepts include **Shinpai suna:** Do not worry,

Kyo dake wa: Today only, **Kansha shite:** Be grateful, **Ikaru na:** Do not anger, **Hito ni shinsetsu ni:** Show compassion, and **Gyo o hageme:** Practice diligently.

Step 4: Close your eyes and place your palms on your head. Chant shlokas and think about Ki (life force energy). Hover your hands over your body by keeping them a couple of inches apart. The movements should be slow and coordinated. Hold until you feel warmth over the spot. Open your eyes slowly and feel the positive changes.

Once the session is over, you may experience tingling sensations in your body, which is a positive sign indicating that your body is healing. Even though it is advised to approach a Reiki master to get attunements, you can try practicing Reiki at home. Since everyone is believed to possess healing energy and Reiki within them, the practice tends to work if performed in the right way. Learn more about chakras and their relation to Reiki baths to try the practice at home.

Reiki Techniques

While the steps mentioned above are the recognized ways of conducting a Reiki session, some practitioners also take distinct approaches based on the case and expectations of the individual.

Reiki with Crystals

Healing crystals are often used by Reiki masters or practitioners and are known to emit positive vibrations and stimulate a person's surroundings. Crystals can enhance the process of pulling out negative energy from one's body and supplying positive vibrations for physical, mental, and spiritual healing. Depending on the case, Reiki masters may hold the crystal in their hand while performing the technique or place one on the person's body. Even though there are no apparent studies to support the effectiveness of crystals, the positivity felt after using crystals has convinced Reiki practitioners to use them during their practice. Some crystals used for Reiki are topaz, rose quartz, moonstone, amethyst, aquamarine, and tourmaline.

Reiki from a Distance

Experienced Reiki masters can conduct a session from a distance by chanting prayers and mantras. While healing from a distance may sound a bit ludicrous, it has been known to work. The fundamental principle of Reiki is gathering the universe's positive frequencies and sending them your way. Whether it's done in close proximity or from a distance, Reiki is known to channel energy through a person's body and hit the chakra spots for effective healing. When treating from a distance, Reiki masters use symbols and mantras to heal an individual. At times, deep meditation and breathing techniques are also a part of the session. The distinctive process focuses on the physiological measures and not on the outcome.

Reiki Beaming

Introduced by the International Center for Reiki Training, this technique involves channeling a beam of energy from a distance to cleanse the individual's aura. The hands of the practitioner act as a receiver that harnesses energy from their surroundings and send it to the individual through a dedicated beam. Some masters also send the energy beam through their eyes or pupils. This technique can be a bit difficult to master. However, with time and practice, the strength of this practice can produce more effective results.

Who Is It Meant For? What Can One Expect?

Reiki is completely safe and non-invasive. Even though there are no plausible side effects connected to Reiki healing, you must consider your physical and mental health before delving into this domain. If you are undergoing any medical treatment, you cannot simply switch it to Reiki. Talk to your doctor before taking any further steps. Several cases of "healing crises" have, however, been noted in the past. This is when a person is affected by an overwhelming flow of energy that amplifies the detox reaction and resulting in their mind and body going into panic mode. Reiki practitioners believe that these situations should be considered a positive sign since they show the efficacy of the healing session. When releasing negative energy and detoxifying, the person may feel nauseous or experience headaches. Other symptoms such as crying and back pain have also been noted.

These signs should not be confused with usual tiredness. While feeling a bit low or tired can be a sign of overworking or fatigue, heavier symptoms such as headache or intensive crying are calcified signs of releasing toxic energy from the body. These signs are temporary and usually fade away within 2 to 24 hours. Meanwhile, your body prepares itself for healing while commencing in the process. This is mainly why many people feel delayed relief after undergoing a Reiki session. After a session, you may instantly feel more relaxed and at peace. As mentioned, you may even have tingling sensations in your body. You could feel energized or tired. It is necessary to drink lots of water immediately after a session.

The effects of Reiki can be mild to intense and vary from person to person. It also depends on the person's physical and mental condition and the amount of healing they need. Several patients who underwent intensive sessions of Reiki before cardiac catheterization, though, felt more courageous and confident. If you are feeling anxious, depressed, or low, Reiki is definitely meant for you. It also helps you counterbalance your past experiences and better prepares you to embrace the future. People with low confidence and low self-esteem should also undergo this practice once to experience its positive effects. Some individuals have also deemed it a life-changing experience.

It is easy to find a Reiki master today. A simple web search can point out several experienced Reiki practitioners in your area. Before appointing one or booking a session, it is important to check reviews and pricing. Make sure that the Reiki master is also renowned and experienced, as it can impact your health negatively if they don't know what they're doing. Individuals seeking treatment from inexperienced Reiki masters have been known to undergo invasive treatments, which can be dangerous. When it comes to Reiki, word-of-mouth recommendations are the best, as the person can attest from real-life experiences and the effects they feel after each session. Some massage clinics and yoga studios may also have contacts of Reiki practitioners.

If you feel uncomfortable with the practitioner of your choice, it is imperative that you stop practicing with them. Since Reiki is about healing and feeling at peace, you should not be stressed or uncomfortable when going through the process. This makes choosing an ideal practitioner even more important. The prices can also hugely differ, which is why you must compare them before appointing a master.

Reiki for a Self-Practitioner

You can practice Reiki at home as well. If you are unable to find an experienced Reiki practitioner in your area, you can teach yourself and practice it at home. All you need to do is find an experienced Reiki master and follow an attunement process. The attunement process enables a body to both receive and transmit energy to or from another being. It is an extremely valuable skill to pick up as your body should have this ability for its entire life. Since no formal education, experience, or specific skills are needed to become a Reiki practitioner, anyone interested in this subject can become a Reiki master under proper guidance.

To master the art of Reiki, you must go through three levels of an intensive course. The course collectively lasts for 8 to 9 hours. There is no industry-recognized document or health board license that allows one to be officially recognized as a Reiki master. Yet, several institutes offer certifications. The course usually involves becoming familiar with healing energies and recognizing clients' ethics. When preparing for the attunement process, you must go through an intensive self-disciplining process that includes a fast that lasts up to 3 days. You also need to meditate and release negative energy to make way for positive vibrations.

Take time to assess yourself between each level and the next while delving into the depth of the practice. Each time you must prepare yourself mentally and physically to endure the next level, but also acknowledge the insights and progress you have made so far. You can also take this time to practice and enhance your newly acquired skills. You can ask your friends or family to act as a candidate and practice Reiki on them. You can also practice it on your house plants. Since Reiki transfers healing properties to all living beings, you have a wide range of subjects to practice on. With time and practice, you can master the art of Reiki and possess the ability to heal beings from a distance. At times, Reiki masters are known to treat an individual's misery from a distance. It involves reciting prayers and mantras to send positive vibrations to the individual.

Reiki is slowly gaining popularity in the scientific medical sphere. In fact, a lot of medical practitioners are now prescribing Reiki as a healing technique and consider it a great option for non-invasive therapy to be coupled with medical treatment. Quantifiable and plausible healing effects from Reiki have been noted by clinical studies as well. If you are new to this domain, look for a practitioner in your region through word-of-mouth recommendations or by searching online. To avoid poor technique and practice, look for an experienced and renowned practitioner, as incorrect practice can be dangerous for your health.

Since Kundalini awakening helps a person meet their true self and unravel the divine energy within, it can often be paired with the healing practice of Reiki. While Reiki is used to extract negative energy to heal a person and alleviate symptoms, a combination of Kundalini and Reiki is used to insert positive vibrations into the body to aid in the awakening of the Kundalini energy. Either way, it is extremely beneficial for the person.

Conclusion

Now that you have gained complete knowledge on Kundalini awakening and its relevant aspects, you can embark on this journey with confidence. As you've learned, the process of Kundalini awakening can be extremely beneficial but overwhelming at the same time. Kundalini is strongly attached to various concepts that an individual attains on their spiritual journeys, such as the importance of chakra balancing, Reiki, and third eye opening. All these aspects can slowly and steadily mold the seeker's life and help them attain a fruitful and spiritual journey.

If you wish to develop psychic awareness and manifest positive energy in your life, pay attention to every detail mentioned throughout the book, as they will collectively point you in the right direction.

Let's sum up the crucial points we've learned:

Basics and Benefits of Kundalini: This energy is coiled at the base of the spine and is dormant until you make an effort to awaken it. If you are successful, you will feel an electrifying effect that is caused by the flow of energy throughout your body. Kundalini can be awoken through meditation, breathing techniques, Reiki, third eye opening, balancing chakras, and certain lifestyle changes. In general, breathing techniques are the primary focus during the process of Kundalini awakening. You've also learned the psychological difference between the Western and the Eastern world (mainly yogic), which emphasizes the importance of seeking and amalgamating the spiritual domain when diagnosing issues in humans.

Chakras: The main focal points or energy centers of your body are predominantly known as chakras and govern a certain area of your internal system. The seven chakras are Muladhara (Root Chakra), Svadhisthana (Sacral or Pelvic Chakra), Manipura (Navel Chakra), Anahata (Heart Chakra), Vishuddha (Throat Chakra), Ajna (Third-Eye Chakra), and Sahasrara (Crown Chakra). Each chakra represents different elements, colors, poses, and benefits, once aligned correctly. It is necessary to keep each chakra balanced to sustain your body's functions and maintain your physical and mental health. Certain signs such as pain in specific body parts or some form of mental health issue will dictate the imbalance in your chakra system. You must take the necessary steps to balance all chakras in order to activate them.

Mudras, Mantras, and Asanas: Various types of Pranayamas (the practice of breath control) can be practiced to heal you. It cleanses your mind and soul, along with helping you achieve inner calmness. Those suffering from breathing, lung, and digestive issues should definitely reap the benefits of Pranayama. Focused gaze, or Drishti, can help you perceive your inner being by disconnecting yourself from the outer world. You can perform various forms of Drishti exercises to boost concentration, energize your chakras, and activate your pituitary gland. The third branch of yoga, asana, is your body's posture as you meditate. Various forms of asanas and mudras are performed to strengthen one's physical and mental state. Mantras or holy chants are repeated when performing mudras and asanas to awaken the soul and enhance focus.

Meditation: The primary goal of Kundalini meditation is to cleanse the mind and aura. It helps you become attuned with your thoughts and gives you the courage to face your fears. Additionally, Kundalini meditation has been proven to aid with anxiety and focus issues. Note that the location you choose to meditate in can affect your overall experience. You can also choose a mediation kriya based on your ailment (to improve your heart condition, build confidence, or enhance your spiritual stamina). Pay attention to the mudras and pick mantras that suit respective kriyas. More importantly, have a calm and clear mind to attain meditation.

Kundalini Awakening and its Effects: The process of Kundalini awakening can be an exhausting and extremely difficult process for an individual. The effects vary from person to person, depending on their health and goals. While some may experience a mild headache and random bouts of anxiety, others may spiral into depression or suffer from physical or mental health conditions such as skin disease or eating disorders. Even though meditation and controlling one's diet can bring on the Kundalini awakening process with ease, you have to stay patient and diligent. Lean on your loved ones for support or seek help from a spiritual guru.

Third Eye Opening: The Ajna chakra (sixth chakra) is also denoted as the Third Eye and possesses eternal power. One who successfully activates their Ajna chakra and opens the third eye is capable of grasping intangible visions that push them closer to the true realm of existence. They are also blessed with newfound immense knowledge and intuition. An inactive or overactive third eye can result in a lack of focus or psychic fantasies. Meditation, seeking guidance from your dreams, and practicing certain yoga postures are effective ways to open your third eye. Some kriyas used in Kundalini can also shift the energy blocks hindering the sixth chakra.

Reiki: This traditional Japanese healing process is used to transfer positive energy from one living being to another. Reiki masters use this technique to summon the universe's positive energy and transfer it to a person through physical contact or remotely from a distance. Reiki treats ailments related to anxiety and depression and improves the overall quality of life by using less invasive methods to heal. You can either hire a Reiki master or go through various levels of attunements with an experienced teacher to learn the technique. Reiki can be performed using crystals, from a distance (by chanting prayers and mantras), or through beaming.

You are now prepared to embark on your spiritual journey and unravel a new dimension of being. If you find the information useful, perhaps encourage your friends and family members to gain insights on the benefits of Kundalini awakening as well. You can also practice meditation and seek this path with your loved ones to gain support. Even though the process of Kundalini awakening can take a long time, you must remember to be patient on this arduous yet rewarding journey. You will also be blessed with immense knowledge, peace of mind, and heightened intuition that can drastically change your life for the better.

References

Luna, A. (2020, November 21). What is Kundalini Awakening? (19 Intense Symptoms). Retrieved from Lonerwolf.com website: https://lonerwolf.com/Kundalini-awakening/

Matson, M. (2020, July 21). Kundalini awakening: What is it and how to awaken it. Retrieved from Brettlarkin.com website: https://www.brettlarkin.com/Kundalini-awakening/

Müller, A. (2020, February 27). Kundalini energy: What it is and how to awaken it within you. Retrieved from Mindfully Speaking website: https://medium.com/mindfully-speaking/Kundalini-energy-what-it-is-and-how-to-awaken-it-within-you-a542f8aa39ed

Before you continue to YouTube. (n.d.-a). Retrieved from Youtube.com website: https://www.youtube.com/watch?v=HafXNhE3gqA

Mahesh Prabhu, U. (2020, October 21). Vedic Counseling and Ayurvedic Psychology. Retrieved from Vedanet.com website: https://www.vedanet.com/vedic-counseling-and-ayurvedic-psychology/

The 8 limbs of yoga explained. (2017, November 13). Retrieved from Ekhartyoga.com website: https://www.ekhartyoga.com/articles/philosophy/the-8-limbs-of-yoga-explained

Am, Tarlton, A., & RYT-. (2020, February 10). Kundalini yoga 101: Everything you wanted to know. Retrieved from Mindbodygreen.com website: https://www.mindbodygreen.com/articles/Kundalini-yoga-101-everything-you-wanted-to-know

Breath of Fire yoga: Benefits and how to do it correctly. (2020, November 9). Retrieved from Healthline.com website: https://www.healthline.com/health/breath-of-fire-yoga

Brittany Deanda And, Tzelnic, A., Marglin, E., Deshpande, R., & Asp, K. (2019, April 13). A beginner's guide to Kundalini Yoga. Retrieved from Yogajournal.com website: https://www.yogajournal.com/yoga-101/a-beginners-guide-to-Kundalini-yoga/

Ilse-Marie. (2019, November 1). 4 - 4 breathing technique for more energy - Kundalini Yoga > viva la Vida. Retrieved from Vivalavidalifestyle.com website: https://vivalavidalifestyle.com/4-4-breathing-technique-for-more-energy-Kundalini-yoga/

Müller, A. (2020, February 27). Kundalini energy: What it is and how to awaken it within you. Retrieved from Mindfully Speaking website: https://medium.com/mindfully-speaking/Kundalini-energy-what-it-is-and-how-to-awaken-it-within-you-a542f8aa39ed

Ramdesh. (2012, October 15). All about Kundalini yoga: Pranayama - spirit voyage blog. Retrieved from Spiritvoyage.com website: https://blog.spiritvoyage.com/all-about-Kundalini-yoga-pranayama/

Sharma, R. (2017, June 24). All you Need to Know of the Kundalini Energy. Retrieved from Modernagespirituality.com website: https://www.modernagespirituality.com/all-you-need-to-know-of-the-Kundalini-energy/

The Basics of Kundalini: Awakening our Serpentine Energy. (2015, February 27). Retrieved from Elephantjournal.com website: https://www.elephantjournal.com/2015/02/the-basics-of-Kundalini-awakening-our-serpentine-energy/

What is Pranayama ? (n.d.). Retrieved from Artofliving.org website: https://www.artofliving.org/in-en/yoga/breathing-techniques/yoga-and-pranayama

History of Kundalini. (n.d.). Retrieved from Icrcanada.org website: https://www.icrcanada.org/learn/historicalbasis

(N.d.). Retrieved from Kundaliniresearchinstitute.org website: https://Kundaliniresearchinstitute.org/wp-content/uploads/2020/10/History-chapter.pdf

Eastern body, Western mind : psychology and the chakra system as a path to the self : Judith, Anodea, 1952- : Free Download, Borrow, and Streaming : Internet Archive. (n.d.). Retrieved from Archive.org website: https://archive.org/details/easternbodyweste00judi_0/page/451

Lebowe, J. (2020, February 24). Ego death: Everything you should know. Retrieved from Doubleblindmag.com website: https://doubleblindmag.com/ego-death/

Sol, M. (2016, October 24). Ego death: 7 terrifying and illuminating stages. Retrieved from Lonerwolf.com website: https://lonerwolf.com/ego-death/

Taylor, S. (2018). Two modes of sudden spiritual awakening? Ego-dissolution and explosive, energetic awakening. International Journal of Transpersonal Studies, 37(2). doi:10.24972/ijts.2018.37.2.131

8 benefits of Kundalini yoga you never knew about. (2016, October 26). Retrieved from Egypttoday.com website: https://www.egypttoday.com/Article/4/3184/8-Benefits-Of-Kundalini-Yoga-You-Never-Knew-About

10 amazing benefits of Kundalini Yoga. (2019, April 21). Retrieved from Lamajowellness.com website: https://lamajowellness.com/10-amazing-benefits-of-Kundalini-yoga/

Nunez, K. (2020, July 16). Kundalini yoga: Poses, benefits, steps for beginners. Retrieved from Healthline.com website: https://www.healthline.com/health/Kundalini-yoga

Cameron, Y. (2020, October 8). Everything you've ever wanted to know about the 7 chakras in the body. Retrieved from Mindbodygreen.com website: https://www.mindbodygreen.com/0-91/The-7-Chakras-for-Beginners.html

Editors, Y. J., Shaw, E., Witmer, S. A., & Jeffries, T. Y. (2015, January 9). Intro to the second chakra: Sacral chakra (svadhisthana). Retrieved from Yogajournal.com website: https://www.yogajournal.com/yoga-101/chakras-yoga-for-beginners/intro-sacral-chakra-svadhisthana/

Editors, Y. J., Shaw, E., Witmer, S. A., & Jeffries, T. Y. (2021a, March 12). Intro to the fourth chakra: Heart chakra (anahata). Retrieved from Yogajournal.com website: https://www.yogajournal.com/yoga-101/chakras-yoga-for-beginners/intro-heart-chakra-anahata/

Editors, Y. J., Shaw, E., Witmer, S. A., & Jeffries, T. Y. (2021b, March 16). Intro to the seventh chakra: Sahasrara (crown) chakra. Retrieved from Yogajournal.com website: https://www.yogajournal.com/yoga-101/chakras-yoga-for-beginners/intro-sahasrara-crown-chakra/

Ferretti, A., Shaw, E., Witmer, S. A., Editors, Y. J., & Jeffries, T. Y. (2014, July 30). A beginner's guide to the chakras. Retrieved from Yogajournal.com website: https://www.yogajournal.com/practice/yoga-sequences-level/beginners-guide-chakras/

Snyder, S., Shaw, E., Witmer, S. A., Editors, Y. J., & Jeffries, T. Y. (2015, January 12). Intro to the third chakra: Navel chakra (manipura). Retrieved from Yogajournal.com website: https://www.yogajournal.com/yoga-101/chakras-yoga-for-beginners/intro-navel-chakra-manipura/

Snyder, S., Tzelnic, A., Marglin, E., Deshpande, R., & Asp, K. (2015a, January 1). Intro to the first chakra: Root chakra (muladhara). Retrieved from Yogajournal.com website: https://www.yogajournal.com/yoga-101/intro-root-chakra-muladhara/

Snyder, S., Tzelnic, A., Marglin, E., Deshpande, R., & Asp, K. (2015b, January 19). Intro to the fifth chakra: Throat chakra (visuddha). Retrieved from Yogajournal.com website: https://www.yogajournal.com/yoga-101/chakratuneup2015-intro-visuddha/

Snyder, S., Tzelnic, A., Marglin, E., Deshpande, R., & Asp, K. (2015c, January 27). Intro to the sixth chakra: Ajna (third-eye) chakra. Retrieved from Yogajournal.com website: https://www.yogajournal.com/yoga-101/chakratuneup2015-intro-ajna/

The complete beginner's guide to the seven chakras - goodnet. (n.d.). Retrieved from Goodnet.org website: https://www.goodnet.org/articles/what-are-seven-chakras-comprehensive-introduction

8 Limbs Yoga. (n.d.). Pranayama - the 4th limb of yoga - 8 limbs yoga. Retrieved from https://8limbsyoga.com/pranayama-the-4th-limb-of-yoga/

9 Minute Read, 14 Minute Read, & 5 Minute Read. (2019, September 9). The 8 limbs of yoga simplified. Retrieved from Motherhoodcommunity.com website: https://motherhoodcommunity.com/the-8-limbs-of-yoga-simplified/

Arya, U. (1986). Yoga sutras of Patanjali. Honesdale, PA: Himalayan Institute Press.

Burgin, T. (1970, January 1). Corpse pose (shavasana or savasana) • yoga basics. Retrieved from Yogabasics.com website: http://yogabasics.com/asana/corpse/

Divya-drishti. (n.d.). Retrieved from Yogapedia.com website: https://www.yogapedia.com/definition/5095/divya-drishti

Gyan Mudra. (n.d.). Retrieved from Yogapedia.com website: https://www.yogapedia.com/definition/6444/gyan-mudra

Kundalini Yoga Mantras. (n.d.). Retrieved from 3Ho.org website: https://www.3ho.org/Kundalini-yoga/mantra/Kundalini-yoga-mantras

Mantra. (n.d.). Retrieved from Yogapedia.com website: https://www.yogapedia.com/definition/4950/mantra

Mudra. (n.d.). Retrieved from Yogapedia.com website: https://www.yogapedia.com/definition/5027/mudra

Notes, Y. (2019). Prithvi Mudra: Notebook Yoga Meditation Namaste Notizbuch Journal 6x9 Lined. Independently Published.

Nunez, K. (2020, July 16). Kundalini yoga: Poses, benefits, steps for beginners. Retrieved from Healthline.com website: https://www.healthline.com/health/Kundalini-yoga

Ong Namo Guru Dev Namo. (n.d.). Retrieved from Yogapedia.com website: https://www.yogapedia.com/definition/10603/ong-namo-guru-dev-namo

Pranayama for Awakening Kundalini. (n.d.). Retrieved from Yogamag.net website: http://www.yogamag.net/archives/2000s/2009/haug09/kund.html

Prax, A. (2017, March 2). The 9 Drishti of Yoga. Retrieved from Yogapedia.com website: https://www.yogapedia.com/the-9-drishti-of-yoga/2/9747

Shunya Mudra. (n.d.). Retrieved from Yogapedia.com website: https://www.yogapedia.com/definition/6859/shunya-mudra

The Yoga Institute. (2012, March 1). KAPALABHATI - the yoga institute. Retrieved from Theyogainstitute.org website: https://theyogainstitute.org/kapalabhati/

The Yoga Institute. (2018a, June 8). What is Bhastrika pranayama & It's Benefits. Retrieved from Theyogainstitute.org website: https://theyogainstitute.org/what-is-bhastrika-pranayama-and-its-benefits/

The Yoga Institute. (2018b, June 10). Full breath retention - Kumbhaka Pranayama. Retrieved from Theyogainstitute.org website: https://theyogainstitute.org/full-breath-retention-kumbhaka-pranayama/

The Yoga Institute. (2018c, June 22). How to do ujjayi pranayama, recommended practice, steps and benefits. Retrieved from Theyogainstitute.org website: https://theyogainstitute.org/ujjayi-pranayama/

Varuna Mudra. (n.d.). Retrieved from Yogapedia.com website: https://www.yogapedia.com/definition/6861/varuna-mudra

Vayu Mudra. (n.d.). Retrieved from Yogapedia.com website: https://www.yogapedia.com/definition/6864/vayu-mudra

3HO Foundation. (n.d.). Retrieved from 3Ho.org website: https://www.3ho.org

Cuncic, A. (n.d.). How to practice Kundalini meditation. Retrieved from Verywellmind.com website: https://www.verywellmind.com/what-is-Kundalini-meditation-4688618

Featured Meditations. (n.d.). Retrieved from 3Ho.org website: https://www.3ho.org/Kundalini-yoga/meditation/featured-meditations

Kundalini meditation: Benefits, how to try, and dangers. (2020, August 18). Retrieved from Healthline.com website: https://www.healthline.com/health/Kundalini-meditation

Alpert, Y. M., Tzelnic, A., Marglin, E., & Deshpande, R. (2015, February 11). Mastering the Om: A guide to yoga chanting for beginners. Retrieved from Yogajournal.com website: https://www.yogajournal.com/yoga-101/mastering-om/

Am, Tarlton, A., & RYT-. (2020, February 10). Kundalini yoga 101: Everything you wanted to know. Retrieved from Mindbodygreen.com website: https://www.mindbodygreen.com/articles/Kundalini-yoga-101-everything-you-wanted-to-know

Beck, M. (2016, April 1). How to release what's blocking you in one minute — sherold Barr. Retrieved from Sheroldbarr.com website: https://sheroldbarr.com/release-blocks/

Brittany Deanda And, Tzelnic, A., Marglin, E., Deshpande, R., & Asp, K. (2019, April 13). A beginner's guide to Kundalini Yoga. Retrieved from Yogajournal.com website: https://www.yogajournal.com/yoga-101/a-beginners-guide-to-Kundalini-yoga/

Cuncic, A. (n.d.). How to practice Kundalini meditation. Retrieved from Verywellmind.com website: https://www.verywellmind.com/what-is-Kundalini-meditation-4688618

Hollister, S., Tzelnic, A., Marglin, E., Deshpande, R., & Asp, K. (2018, March 23). Kundalini sequence to awaken the 10 bodies. Retrieved from Yogajournal.com website: https://www.yogajournal.com/yoga-101/Kundalini-sequence-to-awaken-the-10-bodies/

Khalsa, S. K. (2019, March 6). Kundalini Yoga Warm Ups. Retrieved from Spiritrisingyoga.org website: https://www.spiritrisingyoga.org/Kundalini-info/Kundalini-yoga-warm-ups

Kundalini Yoga: Archer Pose. (2015, October 1). Retrieved from 3Ho.org website: https://www.3ho.org/Kundalini-yoga-archer-pose

Moules, J. (2019, September 9). Practice these 7 Kundalini yoga poses and kriyas to focus your mind and balance your body. Retrieved from Yogiapproved.com website: https://www.yogiapproved.com/yoga/Kundalini-poses-yoga/

Nunez, K. (2020, July 16). Kundalini yoga: Poses, benefits, steps for beginners. Retrieved from Healthline.com website: https://www.healthline.com/health/Kundalini-yoga

Bhumika. (2020, March 24). 10 signs that your Kundalini is awakening. Retrieved from Vedicfeed.com website: https://vedicfeed.com/Kundalini-awakening-signs/

Isaacs, N., & Manning, J. (2017, April 6). Kundalini Awakening: Is this Expansion of Consciousness Safe? Retrieved from Yogajournal.com website: https://www.yogajournal.com/yoga-101/types-of-yoga/Kundalini/Kundalini-awakening/

Luna, A. (2020, November 21). What is Kundalini Awakening? (19 Intense Symptoms). Retrieved from Lonerwolf.com website: https://lonerwolf.com/Kundalini-awakening/

Matson, M. (2020, July 21). Kundalini awakening: What is it and how to awaken it. Retrieved from Brettlarkin.com website: https://www.brettlarkin.com/Kundalini-awakening/

10 Things You Can Do to help your Kundalini process — the Kundalini guide. (n.d.). Retrieved from Kundaliniguide.com website: http://www.Kundaliniguide.com/10-things-you-can-do-to-help-your-Kundalini-process

Eden, L. (2018, March 23). Why is a Kundalini awakening so intense #1: — When Kundalini awakens: Support and guidance through a Kundalini awakening. Retrieved from WhenKundaliniawakens.com website: https://www.whenKundaliniawakens.com/blog/2018/3/22/why-is-a-Kundalini-awakening-so-intense-1

Ferguson, D. (2020, July 7). Kundalini Awakening Stages. Retrieved from Yogasanctuary.co.nz website: https://yogasanctuary.co.nz/Kundalini-awakening-stages/

Help Kundalini Awakening. (n.d.). Retrieved from Kundalinisymptoms.com website: https://Kundalinisymptoms.com/info/help-Kundalini-awakening/

Spiritual crisis coping tools — When Kundalini awakens: Support and guidance through a Kundalini awakening. (n.d.). Retrieved from WhenKundaliniawakens.com website: https://www.whenKundaliniawakens.com/spiritual-crisis-coping-tools

Spiritual Crisis Help. (n.d.). Retrieved from Kundalinisupportnetwork.org website: https://www.Kundalinisupportnetwork.org/

Eddie Modestini And, & Ezrin, S. (2016, January 6). 4 steps to master Adho Mukha Svanasana. Retrieved from Yogajournal.com website: https://www.yogajournal.com/poses/4-steps-master-adho-mukha-svanasana/

How to do Padangusthasana: Steps and Health Benefits. (n.d.). Retrieved from Getatoz.com website: https://www.getatoz.com/content/how-to-do-padangusthasana-steps-and-health-benefits/2267

Louise, E. (2020, January 8). 20 powerful third eye affirmations to heighten your intuition. Retrieved from Throughthephases.com website: https://www.throughthephases.com/third-eye-affirmations/

Third Eye chakra crystal healing. (n.d.). Retrieved from Satincrystals.com website: https://satincrystals.com/pages/healing-the-6th-third-eye-chakra

Weingus, L. (2019, May 27). How to open your third eye. Retrieved from Well+Good website: https://www.wellandgood.com/how-to-open-your-third-eye/

A Mindful Collective. (2019, July 29). You can do Reiki on yourself — here's how. Retrieved from Amindfulcollective.com website: https://www.amindfulcollective.com/blog/2019/7/23/you-can-do-Reiki-on-yourself-heres-how

Brown, K. J. (2021, March 25). Denise Woodard of partake foods is revolutionizing the grocery aisle with allergen-free treats. Retrieved from Well+Good website: https://www.wellandgood.com/denise-woodard-partake-foods/

Cronkleton, E. (2018, June 21). Reiki: Benefits, what to expect, crystals, finding a practitioner. Retrieved from Healthline.com website: https://www.healthline.com/health/Reiki

Newman, T. (2017, September 6). Reiki: What is it and are there benefits? Retrieved from Medicalnewstoday.com website: https://www.medicalnewstoday.com/articles/308772

Roberliza. (2021, January 18). Reiki Therapy: Exploring the health benefits of this ancient energy healing technique. Retrieved from Igafencu.com website: https://www.igafencu.com/r/Reiki-therapy-health-benefits/

www.ingramcontent.com/pod-product-compliance
Lightning Source LLC
Chambersburg PA
CBHW070420120526
44590CB00014B/1467